MR OSBORNE'S
ECONOMIC EXPERIMENT

Published under licence 2014 by Searching Finance Ltd.

ISBN: 9781907720789

Typeset and designed by Deirdré Gyenes

Cover illustration by Simon Key

MR OSBORNE'S ECONOMIC EXPERIMENT

Austerity 1945–51 and 2010–

by William Keegan

About the author

William Keegan has been the Senior Economics Commentator of The Observer for many years, having previously worked at the Bank of England and the *Financial Times*. He is the author of many books, including 'Mrs Thatcher's Economic Experiment', (1984) and 'The Prudence of Mr Gordon Brown' (2003). This is his second work for Searching Finance, the first being 'Saving the world?' Gordon Brown Reconsidered (2012).

About Searching Finance

Searching Finance publishes books on economics, finance, politics and history. Visit *www.searchingfinance.com*

CONTENTS

Acknowledgements vii

Introduction 1

PART I POSTWAR AUSTERITY 9
Chapter 1 Attlee and Cripps – A Personal Loan that led to a
Premiership 11

Chapter 2 Grants and Loans to finance War and Recovery..........15

Chapter 3 Years of Shortages and Rationing 29
Notes: chapters 1–3 34

PART II AUSTERITY IN THE TWENTY FIRST CENTURY 37
Chapter 4 Enter Mr Osborne and Governor Carney................. 39
Notes 43

Chapter 5 Treasury and Bank Policy at Odds 45
Notes 51

Chapter 6 The Limits to Monetary Policy.........................53
Notes 61

Chapter 7 Panic Stations 63
Notes 67

Chapter 8 How to Delay a Recovery............................... 69
Notes 75

Chapter 9 Economies Recover – Eventually 77
Notes 82

Part III Austerity – The Osborne Experiment 85

Chapter 10 An Obsession with Deficits 87
Notes 93

Chapter 11 A Crisis Aggravated by Housing Shortages 95
Notes 99

Chapter 12 What About the Workers? 101
Notes 109

Chapter 13 The Importance of the Exchange Rate 111
Notes 116

Chapter 14 Keynesians versus The Rest 119
Notes 125

Chapter 15 Bubbling House Prices 127
Notes 130

Chapter 16 Interest Rate Dilemmas 133
Notes 137

Conclusion.. 139
Notes 146

Index 149

ACKNOWLEDGEMENTS

I should like to thank all those patient friends and contacts who have helped me with this book, not least Dr Jon Davis and fellow members of the Mile End Group, who always came to the rescue when I was stuck. Tim Nichols, now at the TUC but then at the Child Poverty Action Group was most helpful, as, although she did not know it at the time, was my colleague Polly Toynbee, with her many articles on social developments. Once again, I must single out the remarkable assistance I am lucky enough to receive from my part time secretary Linda Knights, who puts the output from my 1960s typewriters into the computer and is always good humoured.

With regard to those friends who have kindly subjected themselves to reading and commenting on the manuscript, I like to spread the burden with each successive book. On this occasion the short straws were drawn by: Andrew Adonis, Adrian Hamilton, my brother Victor Keegan, Simon Lewis, Bill Martin, Adam Raphael, and Steve Richards. The old friend who drew several short straws and made a quite remarkable contribution to my approach was Alastair Macdonald, whose keen eye combines the experience of Fleet Street and the civil service. However, as usual, the buck stops with the author.

*This book is dedicated to the memory of
Ian Gilmour and Wynne Godley*

INTRODUCTION

THERE HAVE BEEN two periods in the UK since the Second World War to which the label 'austerity' has been applied. The first was under the Attlee Labour governments of 1945–51, and the second under the premiership of David Cameron and chancellorship of George Osborne, from May 2010.

The word 'austerity' connotes different things, to different people, at different times. The periods 1945–51 and 2010 –2014 have been very different indeed, one following wartime devastation and the other financial devastation, with the latter occurring from a starting point of a much higher standard of living.

Under the Attlee governments of 1945 to 1951, Britain was recovering from the huge toll imposed by the costs, both physical and financial, of the Second World War. The spending power of the population had been deliberately restricted by the Coalition government in order to concentrate resources on the war effort. As troops, airmen and sailors were demobilised, and civilians working in armaments factories became redundant, there was a vast redeployment of the labour force.

These men and women were earning money in peacetime occupations, but it was to take years to rebuild a peacetime, productive economy. There were shortages of goods and services, and the state of the nation's finances was so precarious that imports were severely limited. There was nothing like the profusion of imported goods or food that people take for granted today. Taxes were levied not just to finance government spending, but also to keep a firm lid on consumer demand and control the natural tendency for inflation to rise when there is, literally, 'too much money chasing too few goods'.

The war may have been won with the help of allies, and Britain may have warded off a threatened invasion. But from being an imperial power, the nation had been reduced to near bankruptcy, and suffered severely when the Americans abruptly cut off the financial assistance known as Lend Lease shortly after the war ended.

We as a nation became heavily dependent on the new American Loan negotiated by the great economist Lord Keynes in 1945 shortly before his death. We also required the benefit of our share of the Marshall Plan funds, which the US government offered to Western Europe in 1947, after a devastating winter added to Europe's other problems and caused concern in Washington about the threat from communism.

Both the Second World War and the 2007–09 financial crash were, in their different ways, economic cataclysms. But the appropriate policy reactions were very different.

What has been called an 'Age of Austerity' was an era of controls and ration books. This was altogether different from the situation that confronted British and eurozone governments in the face of the financial crisis of 2007 onwards, when the banking system, after the excesses of the boom years, was seen to be itself bankrupt, requiring government support on a massive scale to rescue it and ward off devastating effects on the economy.

The banking crisis induced a collapse of economic demand which needed to be offset by government action, not reinforced by budgetary cuts. A myth was propagated by Chancellor George Osborne and others that it was government deficits that caused the crisis. In fact, it was the banking crisis that caused the rise in public sector deficits, which were the counterpart of the collapse of demand. Policies of austerity were the last thing the British and other European economies needed, as I hope to show in the following pages. That there was an eventual economic recovery does not justify the fiscal policies pursued from the summer of 2010. If the historical pattern of growth had been allowed to continue, output in the UK would have been up to 20 per cent higher in 2013–14 than proved to be the case.

In the course of writing this book, I have had many interesting conversations with people from all walks of life, from the top policymakers to passers-by during my regular strolls around the grounds of Kenwood House in North London. Few disagree that there has been a perceptible increase in poverty and hardship in recent years, and this impression is certainly borne out by the testimony of the Child Poverty Action Group, the Joseph Rowntree Trust, the churches, the good men and women who give time to advising the hard -pressed at many a Citizens' Advice Bureau, and, manifestly, those who organise food banks. A detailed analysis of the general squeeze on living standards on various social groups was made by the Institute for Fiscal Studies in July 2014, based on figures from the Office for National Statistics for the period since the onset of the financial crisis in 2007–08.

It would be misleading, and naive, to blame the manifest increase in social problems entirely on the austerity policies of the government. It is a commonplace that there has now been a long period during which real earnings and living standards have either fallen or remained depressed for large swathes of the population. There has been a kind of unintentional and unexpected 'trade-off' during the crisis and delayed economic recovery between employment and earnings. Unemployment, while still unpleasantly high, did not rise as much as forecasters expected, given the decline in demand, while pay levels were depressed. Thus the long-held assumption of policymakers that having a job was a way out of poverty is no longer valid. Productivity – output per head – has not risen in the way the lessons of previous experience might have suggested, and competition from the impact of 'globalisation' has added to the impact of the emasculation of trades unions.

My contention is not that the policy of austerity is responsible for everything that has gone wrong in the progress, or lack of it, of real earnings and living standards in recent years, but that it has played a considerable part in aggravating the problem: moreover, the concentration of the austerity measures on the public services has caused hardship and misery for the 'voiceless'.

As the veteran economist Robert Neild (a former Chief Economic Adviser to the Treasury) wrote shortly after George Osborne's 'emergency Budget' of 2010: "Confidence, or lack of it, is at the core of the economic crisis. Mr Osborne justified his harsh and urgent budget tightening in June 2010 by the need to maintain confidence and avoid a threat to our sovereign debt. But that budget policy, together with the uncertainty of the business outlook abroad, has undermined the confidence of our businessmen and has led us into depression. They need to have confidence in the future demand for their products if they are to invest in new buildings and machinery and so generate more employment. But that confidence has been squeezed out of them for the sake of foreign confidence".

In 2010, in the wake of the financial crisis, gross government debt as a percentage of GDP was 80 per cent in the UK, lower than in France or Germany. During the austerity period after the Second World War the ratio was 238 per cent in 1947. After decades of economic growth it was reduced to 25 per cent by 1992.

Although much has been made of 'Labour's Mess', government debt, as a share of GDP, was lower in the UK during 2007 than in every other G7 country except Canada. What happened was that in the early period of Brown's Chancellorship there was if anything an over-emphasis on 'prudence', the memory of which, ironically, returned to haunt Brown in the later years. As a matter of plain fact, on the eve of the 2007–08 financial crisis, public spending as a share of the economy was, at around 39 per cent of GDP, close to the levels recorded during the latter years of Kenneth Clarke's 1993–97 Chancellorship.

The fiscal squeeze was supposed to be counterbalanced by monetary policy, via lower interest rates. But as the *Financial Times* commentator Martin Wolf pointed out in the 2013 Wincott Lecture about the period of several years of 'flatlining': "Monetary policy clearly and decisively failed to promote recovery. Animal spirits were completely destroyed. Demand fell. It was a machine designed to fail."

I have often come across economists, politicians and lay members of the public who believe that the other principal contributing factor was that the fiscal policy was relaxed – a typical comment is that "Osborne's bark is bigger than his bite" or "behind the rhetoric he has been quietly Keynesian."

But the Office for Budget Responsibility (OBR) has repeatedly maintained that the stretching of budgetary consolidation into the future does not reflect deliberate policy decisions to ease the squeeze, but, rather, the way in which, until relatively recently, growth was slower than forecast, with a consequent impact on revenues.

It is difficult to reconcile George Osborne's boast to the American Enterprise Institute on 11th April 2014 with a deliberate easing of fiscal policy. He stated on that occasion: "The pace of our fiscal consolidation over the last four years has been steady, with an average annual reduction in the cyclically adjusted primary balance of around 1.6 per cent of GDP – according to the IMF – the largest and most sustained of any major advanced economy."

Of course, once economists and politicians become involved in adjustments for 'the cycle' all manner of disagreements can arise about the measurement of the economic or business cycle and the appropriate 'adjustments' to be made. As Robert Chote of the OBR has pointed out, much depends on the scale of "the structural hit" – or permanent damage that may have been caused by the crisis. The scale of what is euphemistically referred to as the 'consolidation' of the public finances depends, as Mr Chote has conceded, "on highly uncertain estimates of potential GDP."

Also, those who wonder whether complaints about austerity have been overdone can observe that public spending has continued to grow in some areas. But a detailed OBR assessment indicated that public expenditure was budgeted to increase between 2010–11 and 2014–15 in only five Whitehall departments and to be cut in 17. The rhetoric about 'welfare' from Ministers can give the impression that this is the principal target of austerity policies; but the OBR emphasises that the squeeze has been, and is, on public services in general. Paradoxically, there can be mean-minded and bureaucratically insensitive cuts in welfare spending on individuals, coinciding with an overall increase in spending. For instance, the OBR calculated that that between 2009–10 and 2012–13 government spending on 'Disability' went up, by 0.1 per cent of GDP. But between the onset of the financial crisis and 2012–13 there had been a 10 percent increase in the number of people claiming disability payments.

A pithy summary of the interaction between the sluggishness of the recovery and the continuing failure of the Coalition to achieve its targets for deficit reduction – thereby giving the impression to some that the Chancellor has been quietly softening the squeeze – was provided by the National Institute of Economic and Social Research (NIESR) in July 2012. "The UK's poor growth performance over the past two years owes much to coordinated fiscal contraction, here and in the eurozone. Slow growth has in turn made it much more difficult to reduce deficits."

Any illusions that he was not serious about austerity were surely shattered by George Osborne's major speech to the Conservative Party conference in October 2013, in which he unveiled a seven-year plan to achieve an 'absolute' budget surplus before the end of the decade.

He promised further substantial cuts in spending on the public services in particular and 'welfare' in particular. (Personally I have always preferred the older term, 'social security', which gives a better indication of what the social settlement during those early post-war years of austerity was all about.) The strategy was mapped out in detail in the March 2014 Budget.

One final point: members of the Coalition sometimes maintain that they were only building on a deficit reduction strategy inherited from Labour. Thereby hangs a tale: my strong impression is that Gordon Brown, the Prime Minister who had played such a leading role in 'saving the world' in 2008–09, was unhappy about Alistair Darling's last Budget in 2010, because Darling appeared to have been captured by the Treasury view, and was embarking on a fiscal consolidation that was premature. These are deep waters. But what cannot be denied is that the British economy was recovering in mid-2010 and then 'flatlined'. It is my belief that George Osborne's initial pronouncements set the recovery back by several years, with the consequences covered in this book.

PART I

AUSTERITY IN THE POST-WAR YEARS

CHAPTER 1

ATTLEE AND CRIPPS

A PERSONAL LOAN THAT LED TO A

PREMIERSHIP

WHEN I TOLD an economist friend that I was writing a book comparing and contrasting austerity in the immediate post-war period and austerity after 2010, he remarked rather waspishly "This is <u>not austerity</u>."

This, by the way, was an economic commentator who, like me, had been critical of the Cameron-Osborne government's strategy of trying to rein back the budget deficit faster than either of us thought appropriate at a time of economic depression – an approach that, both in Britain and in the eurozone, has long since been described as 'the economics of austerity'.

What my friend meant was that general living standards now are much higher than they were in the 1940s, and that, although many people have suffered hardship as a result of what we both regarded as economically unjustified 'cuts', the way of life of the vast majority of the British population remains much more comfortable, indeed <u>prosperous</u>, than it was in 1945–51. Similarly, although, in common with the National Institute of Economic and Social Research (NIESR), I myself have used the term 'depression' to describe a situation where we have experienced a prolonged period of below potential output, this was a depression at a much higher starting level than in the early 1930s.

11

Moreover, if there is one startling difference between austerity then and austerity more recently, it is that the hard times of the immediate post-war years were shared by the vast majority of the population. By contrast, since the onset of the financial crisis of 2007–08, and what I regard as the inappropriate, indeed counterproductive policies adopted by the Coalition, the hardship, in Britain at least, has been confined to a minority of the population, and many people have, to use that oft-quoted phrase of Macmillan's, 'never had it so good.' Indeed, the visitor to central London could have been forgiven for wondering what all the fuss is about, as he sees people carousing at almost every corner of the Covent Garden and Soho areas.

The word 'austerity' comes, like so many terms used in economic discussion, from the ancient Greek – a language I studied at school before turning to – well, economics. The Greek 'austeros' meant 'harsh' or 'drying'. Interestingly, those Cabinet colleagues who opposed her harsh economic policies of the early 1980s were dismissed contemptuously by Mrs Thatcher as 'Wets', while the colleagues who supported her were known as the 'Dries'.

The British politician who was most associated with the word 'austerity' was Sir Stafford Cripps, Chancellor of the Exchequer under Clement Attlee's premiership, from 1947 to 1950. Cripps himself had no alternative but to preside over a period of real austerity and hardship. But it also suited his personality to make a virtue of austerity, both nationally and personally, even though he himself was comparatively well off. It was arguable whether Mrs Thatcher, with her policies of the early 1980s, was right to claim that there was 'no alternative'. But in 1945–51 there was no alternative to austerity.

The austere Sir Stafford enjoyed a prosperous career at the Bar in the 1930s. Indeed, he was able to come to Attlee's rescue financially when the latter was contemplating giving up politics because he could not afford to finance the duties of the deputy leadership of the Labour Party. This was in December

1933, when the Labour leader George Lansbury was taken
ill and Attlee assumed the temporary role of leader of the
Parliamentary Labour Party. Attlee actually wrote to Cripps,
whom many thought of anyway as a strong candidate for the
leadership, saying that, because of his financial problems "I
think that the only thing for me to do is to resign my position
as temporary leader and for you to take over." Cripps replied
that he would give the Party "a special donation of £500 to be
used as salary for the Deputy Leader until the Leader is fit to
resume his duties."

According to Attlee's biographer Kenneth Harris, this was
the sum that Attlee had calculated as his 'shortfall' for the year:
he had been borrowing from his family firm, and Cripps's
donation more than covered the amount he needed to repay.
For Cripps, a rich man with a flourishing practice, this was
a simple, but nevertheless generous gesture. "I shall of course
easily earn this sum by non-attendance at Executive meetings
etc.", he wrote, implying more attendance at the Law Courts.

This was a crucial moment in Attlee's career. Kenneth
Harris, who interviewed Attlee many times over the years,
concluded that "without this timely help it is unlikely that he
would have become Prime Minister." And, although there were
many difficult moments in Attlee's relationship with Cripps in
subsequent years, including episodes when Cripps supported
efforts by his colleagues to unseat Attlee from the premiership,
from Attlee's point of view that vital help in 1933 outweighed all
subsequent attempts at subversion.

As Cripps's biographer Peter Clarke has written: "Attlee and
Cripps, though never intimates, developed a mutual respect
that sustained political cooperation, on and off, for twenty
years." The man who was to become post-war Prime Minister
to Cripps's Chancellor had told the latter in 1933: "Personally I
think that you are the man who ought to be leading the Party
in George Lansbury's absence and should he not return you
would be his natural successor." Many of his colleagues were

to underestimate Attlee, but not Cripps, who once remarked of the older man – Attlee was seven years his senior – "such a first class brain."

At the time of his financial hardship and Cripps's by no means austere offer of help, Attlee said that he would be prepared to step down from the acting leadership role "at any time." The mutual admiration society had a little local difficulty in 1935, when Lansbury finally resigned and Attlee became a 'stopgap' leader. At this stage Cripps actually supported the London County Council leader Herbert Morrison for the leadership. But Attlee remained permanently grateful to Cripps for what Peter Clarke concluded was "his frankly more valuable financial support."

Cripps was a left-wing intellectual, whose interest in planning suited a period of austerity. He had even had first-hand experience of a planned economy as ambassador to the USSR for a period during the war. As Neil Kinnock observed many years later, "rich intellectuals can afford to be left wing." Attlee, for a long time the Mayor of Stepney, was more centrist, what would now be called a social democrat. A Major in the First World War, in which he distinguished himself at Gallipoli, he had demonstrated his qualities of survival by emerging wounded but in one piece from that 'war to end wars'.

His experience of London's East End left him with a strong desire to alleviate poverty, yet in the post-1945 'shortage' economy it was to be a long haul. He championed some of the nationalisation plans that the left had enthusiastically drawn up for the post-war period, but was not as extreme as Cripps. He understood the workers, but also the middle class from which he hailed – he was educated at a public school, Haileybury. As shown by his need to borrow from Cripps to remain in the running for the leadership, Attlee knew there were degrees of hardship.

CHAPTER 2

GRANTS AND LOANS TO FINANCE

WAR AND RECOVERY

SOME YOUNGER HISTORIANS look back nostalgically on the two Attlee governments of 1945–50 and 1950–51 as a kind of golden era. But for those of us who were living in Britain at the time, the gold was on the distant horizon. Although Churchill was given full credit for his leadership during the war, memories of hardship in the inter-war years were very much associated with Conservative rule and an uncaring kind of capitalism. Much was expected of Labour by the majority of the electorate who had voted for Attlee and his colleagues, but times were tough. The more recent period of austerity introduced by the Cameron-Osborne government was given a fortuitous start by the retiring Chief Secretary of the Treasury Liam Byrne, who made the unfortunate quip that "there's no money left". This much quoted 'remark' was in fact contained in the customary written note from the outgoing Chief Secretary to the incoming one, the Liberal Democrat David Laws. It was clearly meant as a joke, and Treasury officials thought it was bad form for Laws to publicise it. The episode was an echo of the time that the outgoing Conservative Chancellor Reginald Maudling made a joking remark about the sorry state of the books to his Labour successor James Callaghan in 1964. But there was more cross-party camaraderie in those days, and the joke was reserved for their memoirs. Indeed, Maudling and Callaghan got on extremely well.

In fact, by comparison with the situation that faced Attlee in 1945, there was plenty of money left in 2010, and plenty more available. But it was one of those remarks that resonate, and full use of it was made by the incoming Conservative and Liberal Democrat Coalition, in supposed justification of their ambitious strategy of deficit reduction, which turned out to be a strategy for growth reduction.

Britain was faced in 1945 with a chronic balance of payments problem. The war had bled the UK's finances dry.

The country had in fact run a deficit on overseas trade before the war, the balance being struck by her vast inflows of income from overseas investment, not least around the empire. However, such had been the rundown in the nation's overseas assets in order to finance the war effort that by 1946 investment income from overseas was running at less than half the pre-war rate. Moreover, the terms of trade had deteriorated markedly – that is to say the price of imports had increased fourfold. Economists calculated that, in order to balance the books, exports would need to rise not only to pre-war levels, but to some 75 per cent above those levels.

Indeed, it is difficult to envisage how Britain could have survived the war without the financial assistance received under the 'Lend Lease' Agreement. This was the result of intense negotiations between the British and US governments in 1941, with the celebrated British economist Lord Keynes playing a leading role. Keynes was, and is, known throughout the world for his contributions to economic theory and practice – not least for being the father of 'Keynesian economics' and his essential insights into policies for emerging from an economic depression. But he was also a very active participant in the British Treasury during, and immediately after, the war.

Churchill described the funds made available under Lend Lease as "the most unsordid act"; and Britain certainly needed the money. But, as shown in the biographies of Keynes by Roy Harrod, as well as many other sources, this was a most fraught affair, one of several elements in the arduous wartime and immediate post-war negotiations that took its toll on Keynes's health; and, from the national point of view, there can be little doubt that Washington extracted its pound of flesh from Britain, insisting on what was known in euphemistic terms as a 'consideration', to be negotiated in due course, but whose form was destined to cause a major crisis for the Attlee government, and, indeed to contribute to the demise of the British Empire.

Libraries of tortuous detail have been filled outlining the comings and goings, and the many drafts and counterdrafts, surrounding the Lend Lease episode. A key moment was well captured by Moggridge when he wrote: "Once Roosevelt had won the election on 5th November 1940, the next question was what form American financial assistance would take. The answer came on 17th December, just three weeks after Lord Lothian, the British Ambassador in Washington, returning from a quick visit to London, told reporters that Britain was 'beginning to come to the end of her financial resources'. The name of the answer was Lend Lease – the provision of supplies to Britain not in exchange for money but acknowledged by some 'consideration' to be negotiated later".

The Lend Lease Act of 1941 specified that the conditions for financial assistance would be "those which the President deems satisfactory". It went on: "the benefit to the United States may be payment or repaying in kind of property or any other direct or indirect benefit which the President deems satisfactory".

The most obvious, but unspecified, benefit to the US was that Britain would be able to fight on. But the benefit, or consideration, to be negotiated consisted of post-war concessions in British economic policy designed to satisfy the strong free trade views of Cordell Hull, the US Secretary of State. Britain at the time operated a trade policy in favour of the

Empire – 'Imperial Preference' – and Keynes, while his incli-
nations were liberal, was deeply aware of the vulnerability of
Britain's balance of payments position for years to come. Yet, as
Moggridge puts it: "The Americans had asked for…an abate-
ment of Imperial Preference and severe restrictions on Britain's
use of exchange controls and quantitative restrictions from the
end of the war."

Keynes fought hard, but had become acutely aware of the
strength of the administration's position and the difficulties
US administrations always have with Congress. President
Roosevelt told Churchill that the Lend Lease document did not
mean what Keynes feared, yet Article VII of the document had
referred to 'agreed action' directed "to the elimination of all
forms of discriminatory treatment in international commerce,
and the reduction of tariffs and other trade barriers."

In negotiations about the proposed post-war economic
order, Keynes was of the view that "Nothing is more certain
than that the movement of capital funds must be regulated
– which in itself will involve far-reaching departures from *lais-
sez-faire* arrangements."

But, while Lend Lease was welcome and provided much
needed relief for the British war effort, the US insistence on
the abandonment of key exchange controls within a year of the
ending of the Lend Lease assistance was to produce one of the
biggest crises experienced by the Attlee government – a crisis
that became known as the 'Convertibility Crisis', which aggravated the atmosphere of austerity.

The Lend Lease arrangement had provided £2bn a year, the
equivalent of a fifth of a gross domestic product of some £10bn.
It came to an end on 21st August 1945, within just over a month
of the general election that swept Labour to power. Hugh Dalton,
Attlee's first Chancellor, spoke of "an almost desperate plight".
There were not, he said, enough resources for the government
to pay the bills. Keynes noted that the UK's economic difficulties
were "entirely due to the war effort".

The Lend Lease Agreement (1942–45) had been destined, in the small print which not everybody had read, to come to an end when the war was over. A Britain that had won the war in conjunction with the Allies, had run down its resources and monetary reserves, and was at the beginning of the long process that became an obsession of senior officials and was known as 'the end of empire'.

Having written an influential pamphlet on *How to Pay for the War*, Keynes had been our leading negotiator at Bretton Woods in 1944, when the Allies combined to try to build an international economic and monetary order which would involve the maximum of international cooperation in everybody's interest. The principal aim was to avoid a repetition of depression, protectionism and fascism which had proved so disastrous in the 1930s.

Although much was achieved at Bretton Woods, with the setting-up of the World Bank and International Monetary Fund (IMF), Keynes had failed in one crucial respect, in a particular negotiation which illustrated the decline of British imperial power and the supreme dominance of the United States. The technical term for what he failed to establish became known as 'the scarce currency clause'. The essential point was that, while other nations would agree to adjust their currencies against the dollar when this was necessary – and it was most certainly to prove necessary in the case of the United Kingdom – the US entered into no such obligation.

In discussions Keynes was up against a formidable antagonist in the shape of the chief American negotiator, Harry Dexter White. As Benn Steil has established, one of White's obsessions was his desire to maintain the international price competitiveness of the US economy. He did not want, and would not allow, the US to be committed to revaluing the dollar upwards, and he saw the Bretton Woods system as essentially locking in the British and other currencies so that they would not indulge in 'competitive devaluations'. According to White, "every country prefers to have its currency undervalued rather than overvalued."

This very issue, many years later, was to become a bone of contention within the European single currency area. As tensions rose about Germany's large balance of payments surpluses in the closing months of 2013, it was the US Treasury that was lecturing the Germans about beggar my neighbour policies. Basically, there was an asymmetry built into the workings of the single currency, just as there was at Bretton Woods in 1944. As Steil writes: "Whether the United States supports fixed or floating exchange rates at any given point in time is determined by which will give it a more competitive dollar." This does not stop successive US Treasury secretaries from intoning the mantra that they believe in 'a strong dollar'.

The White approach to Bretton Woods and the exchange rate is an important part of the background to the Attlee government's austerity policies, because the all-important export drive was bound to be made even harder with an overvalued exchange rate, although the appropriateness of a devaluation would obviously depend on whether enough peacetime investment had been built up to enable the economy to take advantage of such a devaluation.

Amazingly White, egged on by President Roosevelt, was determined to destroy the British Empire. White was much more interested in a US alliance with the USSR, and, although there was much controversy about whether or not he was technically a Soviet spy, it is pretty obvious from the documents that he was to all extents and purposes working for the Soviets as well as the US. White had seen the future, as it were, and it worked, with a US/Soviet alliance and the collapse of the British Empire.

As Steil points out: "While White was unveiling his economic blueprint, the President was laying out his political version, central to which was the dismantling of the European colonial empires" – not least, the British, starting with India.

White's obsession with the sterling/dollar exchange rate went back to pre-war days, and memories of the pound going off the gold standard in 1931. In one US Treasury memorandum he complained in 1938–39, "most currencies drop with sterling and a decline in sterling really involves the appreciation of the dollar in terms of most currencies", thereby weakening America's competitive position.

Lend Lease may have been described by Churchill as "the most unsordid act", but from the US Treasury's point of view, negotiating it provided a chance to end sterling's international role and secure "financial and trade concessions that would eliminate Britain as an economic and political rival in the post-war landscape" and involve "dismantling the structural supports of the empire."

As noted, during the negotiations for Lend Lease in 1940-41 and subsequently for the American loan to the UK, the hot issue was the quid pro quo under which Britain's trading advantages from giving preferential treatment to the Empire would be removed. The issue was clouded in obfuscation, not least because FDR at one stage maintained that nothing could be further from his mind.

White's preference for the USSR rather than Britain as an ally came up against the brutal fact that having been a wartime ally, with Britain, the USSR was soon seen as a threat. The onset of the Cold War in the late 1940s alerted Washington to a possible threat to Britain and the rest of Western Europe – an important factor behind the formation of the Marshall Plan in 1948.

The establishment of the so-called 'Bretton Woods Institutions' – there was also the General Agreement on Tariffs and Trade, the precursor to the World Trade Organisation, aimed at bringing down protectionist barriers and establishing as free an international trade regime as possible – was all very well. Now the British Treasury in general, and its star player Lord Keynes in particular, had to find a compensatory substitute for Lend Lease. No substitute was going to amount, like Lend Lease, to a fifth of GDP. The efforts began with the post-war American Loan, which, at $3.75bn, or about £1bn, was to be repaid over 50 years, beginning in December 1951. Later came Marshall Aid. The loan was extremely difficult to negotiate – Americans did not like the sound of the 'socialist' and 'nationalisation' noises emanating from London. At one stage Keynes had had enough, and a senior civil servant, Lord Bridges, made a trip to Washington on his behalf. And, although the good news was that the loan was set at a favourable rate of interest of 2 per cent, the bad news was that a condition was that the fragile pound should become 'convertible' to other currencies within a year of being approved by Congress, bringing to an end the heavy exchange controls operated during wartime.

Also, while welcome, this was a one-off payment. Thus Lend Lease had been running at £2bn a year, whereas the much fought-over American Loan was £1bn, period, as the Americans say. The associated condition of 'convertibility' by 1947 was premature, and the action soon had to be reversed. Keynes had rightly insisted on the need for foreign exchange controls, given the economy's parlous position. The word 'convertibility' was jargon for the abolition of exchange controls.

In 1945 Britain's exports were running at less than half the pre-war level, because output for civilian purposes had been heavily restricted by the diversion or resources to the war effort. The balance of payments deficit amounted to about a tenth of the nation's total output; much of the gap had been filled after 1942 by Lend Lease which covered some 60 per cent of the £10bn cumulative trade deficit during the war. It was calculated that the American loan negotiated in the closing months of 1945 would finance the deficit for the next three years (the Canadians also contributed). At Bretton Woods the general agreement was that countries whose economies had been badly hit by the war could maintain exchange controls for five years. Now the Americans were insisting on convertibility within one year of signing.

The floodgates opened, and the loan lasted 18 months instead of three years. This was because money held in London by the nations of the empire and others was being withdrawn – an early indication of the 'sterling balance problems' that were to dog British economic policymakers for decades, by making the pound and the level of reserves much more vulnerable than could be accounted for by our trading position alone. Thus a leading economic historian of the period, Christopher Dow, wrote about 'capital flight' in circumstances where there was a worldwide shortage of dollars; and, as the Chancellor of the time, Hugh Dalton, pointed out, "Sterling, alone of all the other currencies of the European belligerents, was freely convertible" so that "the burden of the desperate dollar shortage of so many other countries was simply shifted to our shoulders."

'Convertibility' was suspended on 23rd July 1947 shortly after General George Marshall had made the famous speech in June 1947 at Harvard in which it was recognised that all the European economies were in trouble and, if they came up with the right proposals, the US would have to help them. This was to lead to the Marshall Plan, although it was essentially President Truman's idea, and seized upon by the British Foreign Secretary Ernest Bevin. After the privation experienced in Europe during the bad winter of 1946–47, which had aggravated an already difficult early post-war economic situation, the State Department had been working on ideas for some kind of help for Europe for some time.

The bad winter of 1946–47 had produced a fuel crisis in the UK, with power cuts that were inevitably blamed by a largely Conservative press on 'the Socialist government'. Shortly after the suspension of convertibility, Sir Stafford Cripps was made Minister for Economic Affairs, with the brief to pay "undivided attention to our economic problems at home and abroad". Since Hugh Dalton was still Chancellor of the Exchequer, this might have indicated that there was a limit to which Cripps's 'undivided' attention could be applied. But by November Dalton had resigned and was replaced by Cripps as Chancellor.

If anybody's name, other than Attlee's, is forever associated with the austerity of those times it is that of Cripps. Yet, as Dow points out, the two big 'austerity' budgets – in 1945 and 1947 – were introduced by Dalton, who raised taxes. Cripps's main fiscal contribution was to keep them high, and not to lower them after Dalton had raised them. The November 1947 Budget has gone down in history principally for Dalton's resignation the day after as a result of a trivial 'leak': he had told a friendly Lobby correspondent some of his plans on the way into the Commons, and the correspondent, who worked for *The Star*, an evening newspaper, had proved not so friendly by managing to get a story into the next edition. These days, budget measures are leaked almost routinely, but this was a *cause celebre*, and provoked the Chancellor's resignation.

As Dow put it, resigning over the leak, and at that particular time, meant that Dalton "inevitably went under a cloud". He was associated with the convertibility fiasco and, however necessary the policy of austerity was, it was not calculated to make the Chancellor popular. His final budget was designed, with reserves still draining away, to improve the balance of payments by boosting exports and restricting imports. As Dalton explained: "The effect of these decisions must be, if taken alone and unsupported by other measures, to increase the inflationary pressure by reducing the supply of domestic goods…without at the same time reducing the total of purchasing power." This was a good, honest explanation.

So it was Dalton, not Cripps, who raised taxes on alcohol and the wide variety of goods covered by the old purchase tax. As Dow observed, it was Dalton who directed macroeconomic policy towards disinflation, and who "accepted the heavy political onus" of increasing taxation.

However, it was 'Austerity Cripps' who, as Dalton's successor, had to implement the measures announced in that emergency budget of autumn 1947. This is why he is more associated in people's memories with austerity than Dalton himself. And it was Cripps who was forever associated with the event that has haunted the Labour Party to this day: the devaluation of 1949.

Although the economy recovered – industrial production rose by about 8 per cent between 1947 and 1948, and exports by a quarter, while the policy of domestic austerity meant that consumer spending was flat – the overall constraints were such that events were leading inexorably to the 1949 devaluation. This was in spite of the benefit of the Marshall Plan, which provided some relief after the exhaustion of the North American Loan.

It seems paradoxical that the mighty export drive, combined with import controls, led to the prospect of a current account balance of payments surplus in 1949, yet the pound had to be devalued. Basically, the problem was the dollar shortage, and the lack of competitiveness of the UK and many other countries vis-à-vis the US. Costs in the UK and elsewhere were too high. The UK was financing its deficit with the US via the proceeds of Marshall Aid, which the historian Alan Milward calculated amounted to 5 per cent of the UK's national income during the period 1948–51. This was what was, as the economic historian Charles Feinstein pointed out, "financing the availability of goods and services from the dollar area" – and administered by the Organisation for European Economic Cooperation, the precursor of the OECD.

Thus Marshall Aid had taken over from the exhausted North America Loan, but was of limited duration. And endless import controls would not be in keeping with the spirit, and indeed rules, of the Bretton Woods agreement. As the economist Sir Alec Cairncross, who was advising the Board of Trade at the time, put it: "The issue was not how to restore British trade to balance but how to respond to the so-called dollar shortage...the time to do this was when the recovery of trade was no longer a matter of logistics but depended again on relative prices. We needed to redirect not only British trade but the trade of the sterling area [i.e. principally the diminishing empire and dominions] and of Europe so that deficits in hard currency and surpluses in soft, inconvertible currency no longer existed side by side; and the way to do this was to make hard currency dearer and soft currency cheaper until the first softened and the second hardened into convertibility."

The pros and cons of devaluation were discussed in Whitehall and with the Americans in the course of the first half of 1949, and in the end, as has often happened since, the issue was effectively forced by a drain on the currency reserves. But the timing, August 1949, was determined, according to Cairncross, by the conversion to the cause of Hugh Gaitskell, who was deputising as Chancellor while the tired and ill Sir Stafford Cripps was in a nursing home.

While that post-war devaluation of the pound against the dollar – followed by many other countries –was a necessary international adjustment, the stigma stuck with the Labour Party, which was for years subject to taunts by the Conservatives that it was "the Party of devaluation" – at least until the Conservatives themselves suffered the humiliation of the pound's exit from the European exchange rate mechanism on Black Wednesday – also in the month of September, but 43 years later.

Thus the new Labour government found itself in a very difficult position from the start. It had been elected because it was more trusted than the Conservatives to work for economic conditions that would render the unemployment and social conditions of the 1920s and 1930s a bad memory and unrepeatable. One must acknowledge that the commitment to employment and a social welfare system that protected citizens "from the cradle to the grave" were products of the wartime coalition, and that the eponymous author of the Beveridge

Report was himself a Liberal. Nevertheless, the great war hero Churchill had fought a rather disreputable election campaign, replete with scare stories and slurs about socialism which did not go down well with the electorate. The war may have produced a kind of consensus about desirable economic and social policies in peacetime, but it was Labour that was more trusted to conduct them.

However, the country was broke and the balance of payments position necessitated a period of genuine austerity, especially if the ambitious aims for the construction of the National Health Service and the welfare state were to be realised. This required a taxation policy of restricting consumer spending, even on those goods that might not be in short supply. Even so, the nation deserved some signal that wartime austerity was at an end: thus, having been elected in July 1945, the new government was able to offer a little relief in Dalton's last budget of November 1945, when the standard (what we nowadays call the 'basic') rate of income tax was reduced from the wartime high of ten shillings (equivalent of 50 pence) in the pound to nine shillings (equivalent of 45 pence), at which level it remained until 1951 when, during the Korean War, it was raised to nine shillings and sixpence (47 1/2 pence).

It is noteworthy that the standard rate of tax in those days of austerity for everyone was equivalent to the top rate of tax ruling under George Osborne in 2014. Basically, macroeconomic policy kept consumer spending under control, while the sequence of loans, including the UK's share of the Marshall Plan from 1948 to 1951, helped to finance the Labour government's ambitious plans for the welfare state. The exhausted Keynes observed towards the end of his life that the American Loan he had so painfully negotiated "is primarily required to meet the political and military expenditure overseas."

Whether it was "primarily" or not, the situation was certainly that it was assisting both those overseas commitments, which were being wound down gradually, AND the welfare state.

CHAPTER 3

YEARS OF SHORTAGES
AND RATIONING

DESPITE THE ROSE-TINTED spectacles worn by some nostalgic observers, the late 1940s were a time of hope, and, to a certain extent, confidence, rather than what economists like to call 'consumer satisfaction'. The social reforms, not least the setting up of the National Health Service, and universal state insurance and pensions, offered a cushion that had not existed before for the vast majority of the people. And the advent of full employment meant that, for all the impact of austerity on the availability of goods, the public mood was more optimistic than it had been during the 1930s.

But the initial recovery under the policies of austerity was more apparent in the macroeconomic statistics than in the average experience of day-to-day living. Thus by the time 'Austerity Cripps' took over from Hugh Dalton in November 1947 most troops had been 'demobilised' and found civilian jobs, and industrial production and exports had returned to pre-war levels. In 1947 the emphasis was still on investment and the 'export drive' rather than satisfying the day-to-day needs of the average household. Thus the volume of exports more than doubled between 1945 and 1947, and investment – in new plant, machinery and buildings – trebled. Meanwhile, consumer spending grew only slowly.

Clothes, food and sweets were still strictly rationed. A week's cheese ration from those days would hardly suffice as a 'plate of cheese' on a modern menu. I vividly recall how our mother had to cut a boiled egg in two to serve my younger brother and me. Indeed, when our little sister was born, my brother observed in desperation, "I would rather have had a hen that laid eggs."

It was a very 'grey' period. The prevailing colour of clothes – jackets, shirts, pullovers, socks – seemed to be grey, and it was a magical opening to a new world when the hoardings advertising the film of Henry V, starring Laurence Olivier, was in colour – as, indeed, was the film itself.

Toilet roll was in short supply. Many households had to rely on cutting up newspapers. And newsprint itself was severely rationed. The typical broadsheet was reduced to eight pages.

Not only was the rationing quite severe, many of the goods and luxuries which people take for granted in the present period of 'austerity' were simply not available to the majority of the population. Most people had a wireless – usually so large that, until put right by one's parents, one could speculate about whether there was a man inside reading the news. Television, although invented before the war, was not available until the late 1940s, and even then it was not until well into the 1950s and early 1960s that most households possessed one, often rented. In the 1950s television sets gave black and white pictures, and 'daytime' television was unheard of. Nor was colour TV on offer until the 1970s. The first television in our area of West Wimbledon (London, SW20) attracted such a crowd of gaping children to the pavement outside that the owners of Avenue House installed net curtains to drive us away. In order to watch the Oval Test in the summer of 1950 we young cricket enthusiasts who did not have the money to go to the ground itself would watch in Bentall's department store, Kingston-on-Thames.

The great liberator for the British housewife was the 'consumer durable' – the Hoover, the refrigerator, the washing machine and, much later, the dishwasher. Many housewives in the 1940s washed by hand and used 'mangles' to rinse clothes, before hanging them out on the line to dry. A favourite advert at the cinema in the 1940s was for a lighter, more efficient type of mangle than the very heavy contrivances that were in general use.

The biggest luxury of all, of course, was the motor car. There were so few around in the 1940s that one could happily play football and cricket with one's friends in the suburban streets, with only occasional interruptions.

Many look back on the Attlee government with nostalgia. This is appropriate in view of the reforms it introduced, but it was often one hell of a battle, with the Conservative press attacking the government at almost every opportunity, blaming it for shortages that it could not avoid. And of all the shortages that hit the headlines, the sporadic fuel shortages and power cuts were probably the biggest source of discontent, and of press and public opprobrium.

Successive Cabinet Ministers responsible for fuel and power were the objects of vicious attack and ridicule. Two names that were continually blackened during the power cuts were those of Emanuel Shinwell and Hugh Gaitskell – before the latter became Chancellor in succession to Sir Stafford Cripps in 1950. The winter of 1946–47 was especially severe. Indeed, as noted, its devastating impact on the whole of Europe was one of the influences on President Truman's championing of the Marshall Plan.

'Austerity', after the onset of the 2007–08 financial crisis, was imposed on societies around Europe with a relatively high standard of living, accustomed to taking for granted what those of us who lived through the 1940s would have regarded as the ultimate in luxury. Many young people who wander the streets and go on trains and the underground carrying smartphones and wearing communications systems in their ears would not recognise a society where most people did not even possess a house telephone. As for the restaurants and comfortable cafés now ubiquitous in our towns and cities, these were few and far between, and very basic.

Of course, there was no drug problem in the 1940s, because there were no drugs, outside, that is, the world of the more decadent elements of the very rich. It was difficult enough to obtain cigarettes. English and American cigarettes were usually stored 'under the counter' for 'regular' customers. The visible ones on offer were 'Turkish'. Hobbies for the young were often such simple practices as collecting stamps and cigarette cards; video games were many decades away.

"What the eye doesn't see the mind does not grieve over", so there was no sense of deprivation of all these modern luxuries which had yet to be invented. On the other hand, there were reminders of what had been available 'pre-war' and were still on the restricted list, such as empty vending machines (for sweets, chocolates etc.) on most stations, and the hushed whispers informing women that 'nylons' were available from certain black market characters known as 'spivs'. A higher standard of living was also visible in contemporary Hollywood films on one's local cinema screens.

The emphasis was on 'utility', both in clothes – which bore a 'utility' label, or logo as it would now be called – and furniture. Bombed houses had to be rebuilt as men were demobilised and building materials became available. Those of us whose houses had not been the object of direct hits but which had suffered from the blast of V1 bombs, or guided missiles, had to put up first with canvas as substitutes for window panes and later with 'frosted' glass. We children would indulge in the dangerous game of 'playing' on bomb sites.

There had been a building boom in the 1930s, which had played an important role in the economic recovery from the 1929–32 Great Depression. A typical example was the ribbon development along the Kingston bypass, not far from where we lived. There was nevertheless an acute housing shortage in the late 1940s, mitigated to some extent by the building of 'prefabs', or prefabricated one-storey houses which did not look at all bad, many of which 'temporary' constructions lasted well into the 1950s and 1960s.

One comedian at the time said "There isn't really a housing shortage. It's just a rumour put about by people who have nowhere to live." The shortage lasted well into the 1950s, giving the left-wing Conservative Harold Macmillan the chance to make his name as the Cabinet Minister who presided successfully over the building of 300,000 houses (or flats) a year – a rare example, perhaps, of a British government-inspired target which was actually achieved.

Another Minister who made an early name for himself was the young Harold Wilson, President of the Board of Trade, with his 'bonfire of controls' in 1949. Yet not all rationing was abolished under the Attlee governments, and the Conservatives in 1951 could hardly wait to demonstrate their slogan that "Conservative Freedom Works". Unfortunately there were snags, notably with the derationing of sweets. This led to such an invasion of confectionery shops that rationing had to be reimposed for a time.

One's memory tends to concentrate on the general atmosphere of rationing; but, as Dow points out: "In total, consumer rationing – even at its height, in 1947 and 1948 – applied to less than a third of consumers' expenditure." Within this, however, there was very prominent rationing in certain categories. Thus about half of food purchases were rationed in 1947 and 1948, bread having been subjected to controls in July 1946 and potatoes in November 1947.

Rationing applied during those years to meat, fats, cheese, eggs and sugar, as well as processed food. There was a gradual process of derationing from the second half of 1948, but it was not until 1954, during the Conservative years, that meat, bacon and cheese were derationed.

It is often observed that, despite the austerity, people enjoyed a healthier diet in those days than they do now, so it is interesting to note that items we are constantly exhorted to eat these days, fish, fresh fruit and most vegetables, were never rationed. To that extent, austerity was good for us!

Finally, an interesting contrast with that post-war period and the present day, when there is so much spending on clothes and furniture, is that, for most of the 1945–51 period, clothes and furniture were subject to heavy rationing.

Notes: chapters 1-3

1. *Attlee* by Kenneth Harris, 1982

2. *As It Happened*, C.R. Attlee, 1954. Attlee says of Cripps: 'He brought to our ranks wide knowledge, fine debating powers and a first class mind.' Since Cripps said of Attlee 'such a first class brain' this was a veritable meeting of minds. Attlee goes on to say that Cripps was 'not always a good judge of men' – but presumably Attlee approved of Cripps's judgement when he made that all important loan.

3. *The Cripps Version: the life of Sir Stafford Cripps*, 2002.

4. Sterling Dollar Diplomacy, Richard N. Gardner 1956 is the classic work on 'Anglo – American Collaboration' but …

5. *The Battle of Bretton Woods*, Benn Steil, 2013, is a riveting account of US actions towards Britain which were more combative than collaborative. More recent, on such battles, is The Summit, Ed Conway, 2014.

6. *The Age of Austerity*, Ed Michael Sissons and Philip French, 1963, is a classic on the postwar period, as are *Never Again*, Peter Hennessy, 1992 and *Austerity Britain*, David Kynaston, 2007.

Philip French notes in the foreword to the paperback edition of *The Age of Austerity,* that Clement Attlee, whose achievement the book had tried to celebrate, wrote a review in the *Sunday Telegraph* which was 'sour and oddly baffled.'

7. The various loan negotiations are copiously covered in three great biographies of Keynes, by Roy Harrod, who knew him well (1951), Robert Skidelsky (John Maynard Keynes, *Fighting For Britain,* 2000), and D.E. Moggridge (Maynard Keynes, *An Economist's Biography,* 1992).

8. On the Marshall Plan, two definitive works are: *Marshall Plan Days,* Charles P. Kindleberger, 1987 and *The European Rescue Of The Nation State,* Alan S. Milward, 1992.

9. There exists a profusion of books on the economics of the postwar austerity period, but the one I have found especially useful for this short book is a great work I have valued for years, *The Management Of The British Economy 1945-60,* J.C.R. Dow, 1964.

   Among many others there are: *Democratic socialism and economic policy, The Attlee years, 1945-51,* Jim Tomlinson, 1997, and *Wages And Employment Policy, 1936-1985,* Russell Jones, 1987.

10. Sir Alec Cairncross wrote prodigiously on the period. What I found particularly valuable was his section on the 'convertibility' issue in a late work, *Living with the Century,* 1998.

11 . One could go on, but let us slow down with *The Chancellors,* Edmund Dell, 1996, which covers the chancellorships of Cripps, Dalton and Hugh Gaitskell in meticulous detail, not forgetting Ben Pimlott's magisterial *Hugh Dalton,* 1985 and, of course, *High Tide and After,* Dalton's far from self-effacing own memoirs, 1962. I also found Kit Jones's biography of the economist Robert Hall, *An Economist Among Mandarins,* 1994, very insightful.

PART II

AUSTERITY IN THE 21ST CENTURY

CHAPTER 4

ENTER MR OSBORNE
AND GOVERNOR CARNEY

UNDER THE CHANCELLORSHIP of George Osborne, the most important stated aim of economic policy, right from the start in June 2010, was to bring down the budget deficit. It has been with this in mind that the Chancellor, indeed the entire Coalition, has repeatedly aimed to justify its policy of 'austerity'. Even when, after three years of what the Shadow Chancellor Ed Balls referred to as 'flatlining', the economy showed signs of recovery in 2013, the Chancellor went out of his way to promise more 'austerity', with the emphasis on day–to-day spending on public services.

The contrast with the post-war years of austerity could hardly be more startling. Although the Attlee government also aimed at budgetary rectitude, and was a lot more successful than Osborne in this regard, the most overriding objective under both Dalton and Cripps was to reduce the balance of payments deficit so that Britain could once again 'pay its way' in the world.

When Cripps took over the Treasury from Dalton in November 1947 the American loan had run out and Marshall Aid had been announced, but not yet agreed and distributed. During the period 1935–45 about £1 billion of overseas assets had been sold – equivalent to about a tenth of national income

– and £13 billion of liabilities (the 'sterling balances') had been incurred, equivalent to one and a third times the nation's gross domestic product.

This was a serious crisis. When he resigned, Dalton in effect carried the can for the unpopularity of the Attlee government associated with the fuel crisis at the beginning of 1947 and the convertibility crisis in the summer. When Cripps arrived at the Treasury, one writer neatly summarised the position: "As far as the broad outlines of policy were concerned, he was less an architect than a prisoner" of Britain's near-bankruptcy.

By contrast, when George Osborne arrived at the Treasury in the summer of 2010, he chose to be a prisoner of the Treasury and the Bank of England because it suited his political strategy and the experiment he was about to conduct. His Labour predecessor, Alistair Darling, had embarked on a strategy to reduce the budget deficit. But the new Chancellor was a lot more ambitious, and Darling's strategy – with which Prime Minister Gordon Brown was not happy – was based on extremely optimistic growth forecasts.

Osborne's political tactic, which his Lib-Dem partners were all too ready to go along with, was to blame the economic crisis with which he was faced entirely on his predecessors: 'Labour's Mess', or, in Prime Minister David Cameron's words, Labour's "failure to mend the roof when the sun was shining." It mattered not that both Cameron and Osborne had backed Labour's broad approach to public spending at the time. The argument went that profligate public spending was the cause of the crisis, and the resulting deficit must be removed. This would require several years of 'austerity', and once the deficit had been eliminated, all would be set fair for the 2015 general election. It was, after all, Osborne himself who had suggested, towards the tail-end of the negotiations over the formation of the Coalition, that there should be a fixed five-year term. This was very new to British politics and the British Constitution; among other things, the new commitment would remove the freedom all Cameron's predecessors had enjoyed, namely to call an election at the most politically attractive time – or, at least, a time that might seem appropriate, although 'events' might occasionally prove otherwise.

Osborne's commitment was made during the first signs of recovery from the 2008–09 depression. Unfortunately his first Budget stopped that recovery in its tracks. When making the commitment neither he nor his advisers are likely to have had any idea that there was a possibility thereby of creating, or helping to create, their very own cycle of 'boom and bust'. Osborne's Labour predecessor Gordon Brown had rashly promised to abolish 'boom and bust' and paid dearly for it. But in 2010 the likelihood of another cycle of 'boom and bust' was remote. Yet by spring 2014 the recovery was finally under way, and with a vengeance. Forecasters, from the Organisation for Economic Co-operation and Development (OECD) to Dr Gerard Lyons, a widely respected City analyst, were competing to bid up the growth rate, and more and more people were becoming concerned that yet another housing 'bubble' was on the cards.

The ultimate irony would be if Osborne's commitment to a fixed term meant that the recovery might end in tears well before the expected general election in May 2015. The entire strategy was based on the argument that budgetary tightening was necessary in order to put the economic house in order, and that this would pave the way for a sustained recovery, not the same thing all over again. Yet, for all the regulatory efforts by the Bank of England – which hoped it had learned from its previous mistakes – there was a widespread feeling that the bankers did not 'get it'; that the financial sector was still wedded to its bad old ways and that another financial crisis could not be ruled out. The rapid rise in house prices early in 2014, most notably in London and the South East, was an obvious source of concern.

Yet another possibility was that the British economy could end up, from Osborne's electoral point of view, with the worst of both worlds: the nightmare would be if the recovery in the real economy proved short-lived, with a combination of a slow-down in China and other 'emerging' markets and continued stagnation in the eurozone inhibiting the growth of exports, while real wages did not grow sufficiently to sustain the growth in consumer spending which, as the Bank of England freely conceded, had been given impetus by a rapid rise in consumer debt. The latter had been officially encouraged by the prolonged policy of keeping nominal interest rates close to zero. By spring 2014 the financial markets had become replete with speculation about the prospect for higher interest rates and what this might do to the finances of those who had over-committed themselves at lower rates.

Such speculation was somewhat embarrassing for Mark Carney, the Canadian who had been brought in to govern the Bank of England in a blaze of publicity. To begin with, Carney appeared to conform to Napoleon's requirement that generals should be lucky. His arrival on 1st July 2013 was followed with notable rapidity by signs of economic recovery, those signs becoming more visible by the quarter. But by spring 2014 they had become so visible that, amid the speculation about higher interest rates, Carney felt it necessary to downplay fears that they would rise rapidly, or too high for the comfort of those who had borrowed rather adventurously in the hope that rates would remain at rock-bottom levels.

In a way the new Governor had been hoist by his own petard. He had made much of a monetary policy, announced with a loud fanfare, of 'forward guidance', under which he promised that interest rates would remain very low for the foreseeable future. The idea was to encourage business to borrow for new investment, and people generally, or 'consumers' as economists like to call them, to feel more confident. However, since 'real' incomes – that is, average incomes after allowance for inflation – had gone through a prolonged period of falling and then being depressed, the initial effect of forward guidance was to encourage more borrowing, or 'dis-saving' in economists' jargon.

It would be naive in the extreme to apportion all the credit for the recovery to Governor Carney, for all his efforts to 'talk up' the economy and implement various micro-schemes to encourage economic activity. It was the most famous monetarist economist of all, the late Professor Milton Friedman, who pronounced that monetary policy worked only with 'long and variable lags'. Interest rates had been held low for several years before Carney arrived, and some of the government's and Bank of England schemes to breathe life into the economy had been in place well before the arrival of Carney, who had been portrayed by many, not least the Chancellor, as a one-man 'Seventh Cavalry'.

Notes

1. In his book 5 Days In May – The Coalition And Beyond, Andrew Adonis, the Labour Peer, covers George Osborne's last minute insistence on a five year term. Adonis was deeply involved in the Coalition negotiations, which, in Labour's case, got nowhere, much to Adonis's regret. He was convinced that Labour could have made a go of it.

2. Governor Carney's speeches are available on the Bank of England's web site, and his regular testimony to the Parliamentary Treasury Committee on the latter's web site. Although much was made in the media of the oddity of a British government needing to appoint an outsider, there are few things new under the sun, and, during that earlier period of austerity, in 1943, an approach was made to Graham Towers, the Governor of the Bank of Canada, about becoming Governor of the Bank of England. Nothing

came of it, but in the autumn of 1945, during preparations for the nationalisation of the Bank of England in 1946, Towers was consulted about what form the legislation should take, although his advice was dismissed. (The Bank of England and Public Policy 1941-58, John Fforde, 1992.) The plot thickens: although Carney was brought up in Canada, it has been reported that he has an Irish passport.

CHAPTER 5

TREASURY AND BANK POLICY
AT ODDS

THE CIRCUMSTANCES surrounding the appointment of Carney are fascinating. Since the granting of operational independence over monetary policy (i.e. the transfer of decision-making power over interest rates from the Prime Minister and Chancellor to the Bank of England) by Gordon Brown in 1997, politicians of both major parties had made as much political capital as they could out of the 'independence' of the Bank.

Yet Osborne very much wanted his own man to be Governor; as far as the Chancellor was concerned, it would be independence up to a point. Not to put too fine a point upon it, Carney was the man who, Osborne hoped, would play a major role in delivering a Conservative election victory in 2015.

Osborne and his close economic adviser Dr Rupert Harrison regarded it as a coup when they finally persuaded Carney, after several attempts, to take the Bank of England job, even if some of Carney's erstwhile Canadian colleagues were reportedly glad to see the back of him. Carney's first notable soundbite was that what the British economy needed was 'escape velocity'.

However, early on, during a hearing of the House of Commons Select Committee on the Treasury, Carney managed to break ranks. In the course of a long session after which the political and financial press concentrated on reporting more topical matters, Carney dissociated himself from the official Chancellorial line, by declaring that fiscal policy was actually hindering the hoped-for economic recovery.

In doing so, the new Governor was highlighting the central contradiction in Osborne's economic strategy. Basically, fiscal policy – decisions about the planned levels of public spending and taxation – was in fact designed to inhibit the onset of a recovery that monetary policy was being relied upon to stimulate. This is not to say that fiscal and monetary policy always need to move in the same direction. But on this occasion there was a clear contradiction.

For Osborne and his allies, the austerity programme – cutting the deficit, with a particular emphasis on public services – so far from inhibiting a recovery, was laying the ground for it. The initial argument was that cutting or restraining the growth of public spending would free resources for a spontaneous recovery in the private sector. The vogue word 'rebalancing' was frequently employed to epitomise a strategy aimed at encouraging private sector investment, with the hope that this would also help exports.

But there was nothing like the emphasis placed during the 1945–51 period on an 'export drive'. And, in any case, during those three years of 'flatlining' the performance of investment was feeble.

The Coalition contrived to produce all manner of excuses as to why the real economy was performing so badly and why the recovery repeatedly forecast by the Office for Budget Responsibility during the years 2010, 2011 and 2012 was conspicuous by its absence and then sluggishness. There had been a rise in commodity prices, thanks to the way China and other 'emerging' markets were taking up the slack in world output caused by the recession in the G7; there was the dampening impact on our exports of the crisis in the eurozone – the eurozone and the rest of the European Union constituting our major export market; and there was (would they ever let us forget?) the mysterious way in which 'Labour's Mess' had allegedly caused a crisis of confidence.

Now, it was true that the rise in commodity prices had affected the terms of trade (the ratio of export prices to import prices); and the situation in the eurozone most certainly did not help. But there is a strong case for saying that the really depressing effect on the confidence of business and 'consumers' came from the panic about the 'inheritance' stirred up by the Coalition itself.

Nowhere, to my knowledge, will one find an acknowledgement in a speech by George Osborne or in his reams of evidence to Treasury Committee hearings that the British economy was actually recovering in spring and summer of 2010. The 'flatlining' followed this burgeoning recovery. And the key moment was when, in his first Budget (June 2010) the Chancellor announced a rise in VAT, the earlier reduction in which, by his Labour predecessor Alistair Darling, had been an important part of the fiscal 'stimulus' agreed by the Group of 20 at their seminal meeting in London on 1st and 2nd April 2009. The VAT decision constituted a £12bn tax rise per annum, the equivalent of almost 1 per cent of GDP.

It was plain for all to see that the talk about the need for 'austerity' had a seriously dampening effect on Keynes's famous 'animal spirits'. Business investment not only failed to fill the gap created by the pruning of public expenditure – it fell. In spring 2014 the air in Westminster and Whitehall was replete with governmental championing of new projects for the infrastructure. This was all part of the long-awaited 'Great Recovery'. Yet for three years government expenditure on the infrastructure had been subjected to severe cuts. And this was at a time when long-term borrowing costs for such projects were historically low. It would have made economic and social sense to take advantage of such rates to finance long-term capital projects.

It can hardly be emphasised enough that it was the banks that caused the crisis, not Labour's public spending plans, which, as noted, had been supported by the Opposition in the run-up to the crisis. Labour's public spending plans were not responsible for the financial crisis that hit the US economy, France, Italy, Spain, Greece and other members of the eurozone.

The present government has seldom lost an opportunity to hammer on about 'Labour's Mess'. Yet the record demonstrates that, for all the apparent political success the Chancellor and his colleagues have had in making people believe them, the charge simply does not stand up. Thus Treasury figures show that the key measure, net public sector debt as a percentage of GDP, was actually higher during the last two financial years of the Major government than in any year under Gordon Brown's Chancellorship (1997 to 2007). The ratio was 41.9 per cent in 1995–96 and 42.4 per cent in 1996–97. By contrast, during Brown's Chancellorship, 1997–2007, the net debt ratio was lower than in every year of Kenneth Clarke's period (1993–97) at the Treasury. Contrary to all the propaganda, Brown did indeed 'mend the roof while the sun was shining', with the net debt to GDP ratio falling to 29.7 per cent in 2001–02. It was still only 35.9 per cent in the last year of his Chancellorship, 2006–07. Moreover, the latter years reflected the impact of much-needed investment in education and the health service.

The big rise in the ratio came with the onset of the financial crisis of 2007–09 when, under the Chancellorship of Alistair Darling, the net debt to GDP ratio rose to 43.5 per cent in 2008–09 and 52.5 per cent in 2009–10. This reflected the impact of the recession on demand in the economy and therefore on tax receipts (in particular the receipts from the financial sector, which had accounted during the golden days for a quarter of all corporate tax revenue) and on spending on social security, as unemployment rose by 800,000 between 2007 and 2010.

Such reliance on that particular basket of eggs was certainly unfortunate, but in doing so the Labour government was merely following the example of the Conservatives.

Where governments were responsible, or should we say irresponsible, was in the way that, seduced by the vogue for 'light touch' regulation, and by the belief in the wisdom and 'efficiency' of financial markets, they allowed the financial markets to run amok.

Just as the old-style directors of Barings in London during the 1990s turned a blind eye to the real source of the 'profits' being generated by their 'rogue trader' Nick Leeson, so, one fears, did the Treasury and Bank of England to the implications of what was going on in the City of London. Indeed, in March 2014 Ed Balls, the Shadow Chancellor – who had been Minister for the City at one stage under Tony Blair – owned up publicly to the mistake New Labour made in relying so much on revenue from a financial model that turned out to be deeply flawed.

It was a collective failure, as Sir Nicholas Macpherson, Permanent Secretary to the Treasury (the top civil servant in that organisation) pointed out in an inaugural lecture to the Mile End Group of Queen Mary, University of London. But it was not New Labour that originally championed the deregulation of the 1980s. That was the product of a lethal mixture of the ascendancy of the free market philosophies championed by Mrs Thatcher and Ronald Reagan, and the financial pressure groups that stood to gain from what became a free-for-all, leading to a crisis in which the bankers were bailed out at the taxpayers' expense.

Such was the arrogance and sense of entitlement of the bankers and financial 'traders' involved that, after the rescue, they effectively demanded a return to 'business as usual', awarding themselves huge 'bonuses' even when they were recording sensational losses.

The bankers and traders were skilful at a form of blackmail: if they did not receive their bonuses, they would move to another financial centre. But moving between countries is quite complicated, even in this jet age. It took some time, for example, for Mark Carney to make arrangements to move his family from Canada to London when he assumed his responsibilities at the Bank of England.

The absurdity of the bonus debate was highlighted on one occasion by the man who ranks as possibly the most distinguished central banker of the last 40 years, namely Paul Volcker, former Chairman of the US Federal Reserve Board. A few years ago he said to a gathering of bankers and officials that, when he had suggested action to curb the bonus culture, he had been told that they would move from New York to London. The next day he picked up a copy of the *Financial Times* and read a report that financial operators in London were threatening to move to New York.... Interestingly, that very same newspaper reported on 27th June 2014 the Chief Executive of Barclays, Antony Jenkins, as admitting that he had given higher bonuses, even though profits were falling, in the belief that he could prevent top bankers from leaving the bank, only to see several of them leave after collecting their pay-outs.

Carney himself is on record as having said he was less concerned about the level of bonuses than with the 'structure' of so-called 'compensation' in the financial sector. Perhaps this is not surprising coming from a man with a background in the lush pastures of Goldman Sachs, and who managed to negotiate himself a salary that was more than double that paid to his predecessor, with other fringe benefits.

The extraordinarily high salaries and bonuses in the financial sector continue to annoy many members of the public, the common refrain being "the bankers just don't get it". But they certainly get their absurdly inflated emoluments all right, and seem surprised when one speaks to them that there should be such public disquiet about the huge disparity of income in modern society. One recalls that in Britain, during the 1970s, when the top rate of income tax was 83 per cent – and the top rate on investment incomes 98 per cent – all manner of 'fringe benefits' were thought justifiable in the circumstances. But the marked reduction in marginal tax rates during the 1980s was not accompanied by an obvious move to reduce benefits and bonuses. On the contrary, the 'deregulation' culture brought with it a climate in which executive salaries shot up, ethical standards were eroded and the stage was set for the free-for-all which led to the financial crisis.

Notes

1. Net public debt comparisons are from the Office for National Statistics and HM Treasury.

2. The lecture by Sir Nicholas Macpherson, referred to in this chapter, was entitled 'The Treasury View' and delivered to the Mile End Group on 15 January 2014.

   See also 'The Origins of Treasury Control', lecture to the Mile End Group by Sir Nicholas Macpherson, on 14 December 2012.

CHAPTER 6

THE LIMITS TO MONETARY POLICY

ONE OF THE GREAT occasions in the British economic calendar is the annual Mais Lecture, delivered for many years at the City University, and more recently at the Cass Business School, which is connected to the university. On 18th March 2014 the lecture was delivered by Mark Carney, three years after George Osborne, then Shadow Chancellor, had unveiled his plans, in the course of the Mais Lecture, for bringing banking supervision back under the roof of the Bank of England.

The supervisory role had been removed from the Bank by Chancellor Gordon Brown, after he arrived at the Treasury in May 1997. This constituted a calculated insult to the Bank, which had been associated with a sequence of supervisory failures, including Johnson Matthey Bankers, Barings and BCCI. The loss of the supervisory role was a mixed blessing; indeed there were senior Bank officials who over the years used to confide that they regarded supervision as a losing wicket, because there were bound to be failures from time to time.

The loss of supervision, as well as conduct of the market in government stocks (the gilt office), caused a stir at the time, but was soon overshadowed by the putative success of the 'independent' Bank in controlling inflation. The problem was that, in concentrating nearly all its efforts on meeting, or trying to meet, the inflation target, the Bank took its eye off the dangers associated with the inflation of asset prices and the free-for-all in the financial markets. In practice, the then Governor of the Bank, Mervyn, now Lord, King did not appear to his critics to take seriously enough the fact that, although supervision had been hived off to the Financial Services Authority in Canary Wharf, the Bank itself was still supposed to be responsible for 'financial stability'. An example of this is when a very senior lawyer who had developed an interest in financial derivatives and was given an advisory role at the Bank found that the Governor did not have time to see him to discuss his concerns.

Much has been written about the 'divide and rule' nature of the arrangements devised by New Labour. George Osborne promised a more coherent approach to 'financial stability' when delivering the Mais Lecture in 2010; and here, in March 2014, was King's successor, chosen by Osborne, giving a progress report.

Carney, part of whose brief was 'to shake up the Bank' announced a major reorganisation, involving new appointments, and the moving sideways of some officials with whom he was reported not to get on. In the classic pattern of new arrivals who wish to make their stamp on an organisation, he had hired the advice of management consultants, the well-known international firm of McKinsey. Management consultants are traditionally expected to give the advice that the people who hire them want to hear, but find it easier to cite a second source to endorse their wishes. Time will tell whether Osborne's nominee has produced an organisation that will serve the dual function of ensuring monetary and financial stability. But the complex organisational chart unveiled at the time gave one a strong impression that this, too, was a case of 'divide and rule', offering opportunities for crossed lines and overlapping responsibilities.

The other main theme of Carney's Mais Lecture was that there were repeated references to the risks, in both the national and international financial system, which could lead to another crisis. Thus, although the new Governor made some thinly veiled criticisms of the regulatory regime of his predecessor, he still appeared to be covering his tracks. In particular, on this and subsequent occasions, he manifested concern about the high levels of household debt that still prevailed after the crisis.

However, notwithstanding the importance of the regulatory structure; and notwithstanding the way that entire economies had been derailed by a combination of irresponsible banking and lax regulation, the concentration of politicians and the electorate in the run-up to the May 2015 British general election is likely to be focused principally on the performance of the economy. Banks are certain to remain unpopular – and seem, at the top, to be doing their level best to remain so – but in general fingers are crossed that there will not be another financial crisis in the near term. (Of course, many bankers do not fit into the 'greedy for bonuses while we continue to make losses' category. Indeed, some bankers lower down the scale have suffered from the greed and chaos at the top, and often been subjected to absurd restrictions on their discretionary powers.)

As noted, Carney initially appeared to belong to Napoleon's category of 'lucky' generals. The economy was finally on the turn when he arrived in July 2013, and the new Governor popularised a term, 'escape velocity', to describe what in his opinion the British economy required after its period of sharp decline and then stagnation.

Carney comes from 'central casting' in the sense that he was a follower of the then Federal Reserve Chairman Ben Bernanke, who had been a student of both the Great Depression and the so-called 'lost decade' associated with inadequate and, hence, inefficacious policies in Japan during the 1990s. Bernanke believed in keeping monetary policy as loose as possible in the face of depression. This was to be achieved with the aid of rock-bottom interest rates and the supply of abundant liquidity – 'quantitative easing' – to the financial system.

The term 'quantitative easing' is typical of the kind of jargon with which the economic and financial world can mystify the general public. Although there are all sorts of technicalities involved in its operation, all it really boils down to is an attempt – or, in recent experience, repeated attempts – to expand the supply of money and credit. To this author's mind it is an absurd and ugly phrase, and it was a great moment when someone decided to name a racehorse 'Quantitative Easing'. Indeed my old friend and Fleet Street colleague Christopher Fildes drew this to the Governor of the Bank of England's attention, and Mervyn King referred to the racehorse to lighten the tone of one of his monetary speeches.

That quantitative easing (QE) was for a time the source of great confusion in the financial press amused Lord King who, since his retirement from the Bank, has been known to quip "The only people who did not understand quantitative easing were economists".

The Bank of England had in fact been following the QE approach under Carney's predecessor King. However, Bernanke made no secret of his concern that monetary policy in the US was inhibited by a fiscal policy often operating – after the initial 2008–09 'stimulus' – in the wrong direction. And, as noted, Carney, too, was open about the fiscal constraints.

Nevertheless, economies do eventually recover. This process began in 2013, and, while he was criticised for the apparent emphasis he laid on one indicator of policy, namely unemployment, Carney's concern for the level of unemployment, as with Bernanke in the US, was certainly a welcome sign. Also, while highlighting the level of unemployment as a key target for measuring progress and determining future changes in policy, Carney and the Monetary Policy Committee were well aware that a whole range of economic indicators needed to be taken into account when deciding on the eventual tightening of monetary policy. After all, one generation of policymakers had made fools of themselves by being obsessed with targets for the money supply in 1980s; and another by placing too much emphasis on the consumer price index, while neglecting signs of 'irrational exuberance' in the property and financial asset markets.

Just as it was absurd, although politically advantageous, for the Coalition to blame 'Labour's Mess' for the banking crisis and its consequences, so it was unfair to blame Carney's predecessor Mervyn King for the fact that the Bank of England had failed to prevent that crisis. It had been not just, in Sir Nicholas Macpherson's admission, a collective failure of British policymakers; it had been a failure of the entire Group of Seven economic policymaking Establishment.

There were many strands: thus the regulators in Britain had manifestly disgraced themselves with regard to the lax supervision of Northern Rock; on the other hand, Mervyn King and his colleagues could hardly be blamed for the US subprime crisis, which to some extent, had been caused by official encouragement of loans to impoverished borrowers who were in no position to service them.

Reflecting later on those events, Mervyn King pointed to the irony by which, as a result of his early decision on taking office to spend a lot of time in the regions of the UK, he had neglected to have enough contact with the City of London – a neglect that did not help him when the crisis struck. This is a vicarious lesson that will not have escaped his successor.

Two points strike one about the former Governor's approach in his latter days at the Bank. One is that, in championing 'quantitative easing' he had certainly, with Bernanke and other students of the Great Depression, learned the importance of not aggravating a depression with monetary tightening. For decades the emphasis in monetary policy had been on fighting inflation by trying to control the expansion of money and credit. But when the financial crisis hit, the banks were not lending to one another, and the figures for money supply and credit were indicating a sharp contraction. The point of QE was simply to counteract deflationary forces. Speculation that this was somehow wildly inflationary was very wide of the mark.

There was much debate, under King and in Carney's early days, about the efficacy of QE. George Osborne seemed to regard these operations – known in the old days by the less arcane description 'open market operations' – as 'expansionary', whereas it is probably better to regard QE as a defensive operation, to prevent a freefall in the supply of credit. Economists such as Keynes and his disciple Joan Robinson used to refer to a situation where monetary policy could be compared to 'pushing on a string': i.e. its 'expansionary' impact could be nebulous – and certainly less impressive than increases in public spending which could directly boost demand in the economy and also have 'multiplier' effects.

The concept of the 'multiplier' was an insight of Richard Kahn, a Cambridge colleague of Keynes's. The direct recipients of higher public spending or lower taxes – Keynes himself concentrated more on public spending when talking about fiscal policy – would spend in turn, raising the purchasing power of recipients, and therefore having 'multiplier' effects.

At this point it may be useful to be reminded of the essential Keynesian message, as elegantly summarised by the Nobel Laureate Paul Krugman in his introduction to Palgrave's edition of The General Theory.

"First, economies can and often do suffer from an overall lack of demand, which leads to involuntary unemployment. Secondly, the economy's automatic tendency to correct shortfalls in demand, if it exists at all, operates slowly and painfully. Thirdly, Government policies to increase demand, by contrast, can reduce unemployment quickly. Fourthly, [and highly relevant to the Bank of England's monetary policy discussed in these chapters] sometimes increasing the money supply won't be enough to persuade the private sector to spend more, and government spending must step into the breach."

Of course, under Mr Osborne's strategy of deficit reduction during a depression everything was being done to prevent government spending from stepping into the breach. On the contrary, in the early stages, the breach was being widened.

Osborne appeared to believe that during the early years of his fiscal squeeze, fiscal contraction could be offset by monetary expansion. But for several years QE's function seemed to be one of 'stopping the rot' rather than realising the confident growth forecasts of the Office for Budget Responsibility, to which the new Chancellor had hived off the traditional forecasting function of the Treasury.

The Chancellor often boasted about how clever and responsible he had been in allocating the forecasting machine to an independent body; and, in Robert Chote, formerly head of the Institute for Fiscal Studies, he had chosen a widely respected and most honourable man. I myself often wondered why Chote should want to go from commenting on government policy to making forecasts which could so easily go wrong, and subject him to criticism. But the urbane Chote is nobody's prisoner, and proceeded to make an honest job of explaining why the forecasts had gone wrong; the Office for Budget Responsibility (OBR) would also spell out the implications of the budgetary and wider economic position, with a particular emphasis on an area long widely ignored by the financial markets, namely the balance of payments.

When Keynes and Kahn worked on the multiplier theory, the emphasis tended to be on how an expansionary fiscal policy could have extra impact in raising demand and bringing down unemployment. However, during the period of fiscal contraction which began with Osborne's Chancellorship in the UK, and the reaction of the eurozone's policymakers to the onset of the post-2007–08 depression, concerns arose, not least at the IMF – once assumed to be on the hawkish side of the policy debate – that the multiplier could work equally well, in the opposite direction.

It soon became obvious that Osborne's plan to eradicate the so-called 'structural' deficit by 2015 was not only damaging but also unrealistic. His economic advisers tried to comfort him and the wider economic audience by pointing out that the 'automatic stabilisers' were operating – that is to say, that tax receipts were proving to be lower than forecast on account of the absence and, later, weakness of the recovery, and 'social' spending somewhat higher. Thus the failure of the Chancellor to achieve his targets for the reduction of the deficit was being rationalised as some kind of sensible, indeed humanitarian and pragmatic reaction to events.

We have not quite reached the stage in British politics where Big Brother has taken control of the economic policy machine. We may be a nation whose inhabitants are subject to greater surveillance – all those CCTV cameras – than any other nation in the civilised world (goodness knows how many cameras there are in North Korea), but we have not yet arrived at the point where a latter-day Winston Smith sits in the Ministry of Truth revising earlier forecasts so that they match the actual outturn. Instead, failures to achieve the forecasts are explained by the OBR, rationalised by the Treasury and the Bank of England, and followed by revised forecasts, pushing the achievement of a balanced budget further and further into the distance. The 'structural' deficit was revised upwards because the OBR had recalculated (downward) its estimate of potential GDP. The actual deficit was larger than forecast because of the weakness of the economy. The decline in the size of the economy in cash, or nominal, terms had a dramatic effect on the ratio of the deficit to GDP.

Why did the Treasury and the Bank of England back a deficit reduction plan that in this author's view had been contrived for purely political reasons? We shall try to answer this question in the next chapter.

Notes

1. Richard Kahn: Professor Richard Kahn is far less well known, outside the economics profession, than Keynes, yet he played a vital role in the formation of Keynes's views and work. The 'multiplier' is defined technically as 'a relation between the INCREASE in exogenous aggregate expenditure and the INCREASE in net national product thereby generated (and thus also in employment, if employment is proportional to net national product and the economy is in a situation of unemployment due to lack of effective aggregate demand).' (Luigi L. Pasinetti, *The New Palgrave Dictionary of Economics*, 1987.)

   In the opinion of the great economist Joseph Schumpeter, Kahn's contribution to Keynes's *General Theory* was such that it 'cannot have fallen very far short of co-authorship.' (*History of Economic Analysis*, 1954).

2. Keynes's *The General Theory of Employment, Interest and Money*, was first published in 1936. The Palgrave edition with Paul Krugman's introduction, quoted in this chapter, was published in 2007.

CHAPTER 7

PANIC STATIONS

I WAS HAVING COFFEE one morning at Kenwood, in North London, when I met my friend David Cornwell, alias John Le Carré. When we got onto the economic situation and talked about all the 'cuts' in the budgets of local authorities which were affecting social services, the great man came out with a phrase that seemed to capture the position beautifully. "It's planned penury", he said.

The national press – more the *Guardian*, it has to be said, than the *Daily Mail* or the *Telegraph* – were reporting daily on the misery caused to people at the bottom end of what economists call 'the income scale' by the repercussions of the 'cuts'. The central government was boasting about freezing the council tax, while cutting back its grants to local authorities by 30 per cent. This was a deliberate policy, and it was obvious that it was hurting the poor and the defenceless in particular.

With the support of powerful propaganda in the tabloids, the Chancellor and his close colleagues were contriving to give the impression that a budgetary crisis caused by the failure of the financial system was somehow the consequence of excessive government spending. But it has also become apparent, from speeches by David Cameron, George Osborne and the prince across the Thames, Alexander 'Boris' Johnson, that the underlying policy, the Thucydidean 'truest cause', is their desire to shrink the size of the state. Their allies in the right-wing tabloid press are especially skilful at seeking out examples of 'welfare scroungers' and giving the impression that such people constitute a majority of welfare recipients, yet all the evidence suggests that they are a very tiny minority of the population. And, of course, they had nothing to do with the financial crash and the subsequent swelling of the budgetary deficit.

The broad approach of the Coalition was the reverse of what one had hoped the great economist John Maynard Keynes had taught the world. When the private sector loses confidence and cuts back its spending, then it is the duty of the public sector to fill the gap, not aggravate the crisis by cutting, or restricting, its own spending.

George Osborne and his supporters tried to justify his fiscal policy in a variety of ways. First there was a magnificent oxymoron, 'expansionary fiscal contraction'. A fiscal squeeze was supposed, according to this eccentric way of thinking, to promote an economic recovery either by boosting the confidence and 'animal spirits' of entrepreneurs and high-powered executives who make decisions about future investment, or by 'creating room' for expansion outside the public sector.

This seemed, in the mind of the retiring Governor of the Bank of England, Mervyn King, to be connected with the 'rebalancing' of the economy that he had been advocating for much of his Governorship. There is nothing wrong with the idea of 'rebalancing' itself, other, perhaps, than that it has become a slogan or ritual incantation whose meaning is often lost on the listener. In the specific case of the British economy, it has long been obvious that there ought to be some 'rebalancing' between consumer spending and exports. When one refers to exports it is helpful to bear in mind that a similar effect can be achieved by what economists call 'import saving', that is, a greater effort to manufacture things here that are at present made abroad. In this context, the relocation of investment activities overseas – 'outsourcing' – became fashionable over a decade ago; but more recently there has been some rethinking of the policy on the part of individual manufacturers, giving rise to the term 'onshoring', instead of 'offshoring'.

The phrase economists at the Bank of England and the Office for Budget Responsibility (OBR) use to capture the outcome of the balance between exports and imports is 'net trade', or 'exports minus imports'. Lord King, who gave strong backing to Osborne's fiscal policy, is thought to have justified this by his belief that the impact on demand of the fiscal squeeze would be offset by significantly higher private investment and exports. This, to my mind, did not justify the policy of 'planned penury' towards local authorities and tenants of social housing and the many cuts in housing and other benefits. But, in any case, the Bank of England and the OBR continued, in the years 2010 to 2014, to bemoan the feeble performance of investment and 'net trade'.

So what was the official reaction to the fact that Ed Balls was right, and we experienced three years of 'flatlining'? It was to blame rising commodity prices, for the deleterious impact on real incomes (that is, incomes after taking inflation into account) and the depressed state of the eurozone – our principal overseas market – for our poor export performance.

The government could not do much about rising commodity prices. Moreover, there is a cycle in these matters, and governments are all too willing to take credit for the beneficial effect on real incomes that comes with falling commodity prices. But the irony of blaming the eurozone's depressed state for the poor performance of our exports was that the eurozone countries were espousing the very policies of austerity which Osborne preached, with inevitable effects on the demand for our exports in our principal overseas market.

Also, the idea that the British government required an austerity programme to 'make room' for investment, most notably in the nation's infrastructure, was a red herring: there was already plenty of room in the economy for investment after the collapse of demand that had followed the financial crash.

Just as the build-up to the crash had been accompanied by a collective failure on the part of the policymakers to appreciate what was going on beneath the surface of their success in controlling the consumer price index, so there seemed in Britain and the eurozone to be a collective panic about the right policies to adopt in the aftermath of what some of us refer to as the depression and the ill-fated former Managing Director of the IMF, Dominique Strauss-Kahn termed the 'Great Recession'.

Thus, while there seems little doubt that the new Chancellor in 2010 wished to reduce the size of the public sector, with a particular emphasis on welfare spending, he was firmly backed in his programme for deficit reduction by both the official Treasury and the Bank of England. Paul Tucker, the Deputy Governor who lost to Mark Carney in the succession stakes, told a gathering of the Business Economists Group in February 2012 that, when he saw what was happening to Greece in the financial markets in the summer of 2010, he alerted others to the need for a serious plan to reduce the deficit. Mervyn King's similar views were no secret in Establishment circles. And Sir Nicholas Macpherson defended the Treasury's decision to raise VAT in the summer of 2010 by claiming that he was worried that the UK economy had reached 'an inflection point'.

The Treasury is always concerned about the level of public spending. Such concern goes with the territory: it is its duty to be the watchdog. The Bank of England's statutory obligations include trying to hit a symmetrical inflation target, whereby the Monetary Policy Committee must try to stimulate the economy if inflation is forecast to turn out lower than the target. At the time the new Chancellor came into office, the Bank was maintaining its interest 'policy rate' at the 0.5 per cent low introduced on 5th March 2009 in reaction to the crisis, although inflation was above target. Its sensible judgement was that it could do nothing about the temporary rise in commodity prices, and the last thing the British economy needed in summer 2010 was a rise in interest rates.

However, the Bank has, historically, always been obsessed by the level of government borrowing. More recently the usual talk has been about the size of 'the deficit'. The vogue concern for many years used to be expressed in terms of the PSBR, or public sector borrowing requirement. For much of my career, successive Governors would lecture successive governments about the level of the PSBR – always too high in their view. This made more sense when the Bank was responsible for the management of the National Debt. But this responsibility was taken away from the Bank by Gordon Brown in 1997–98 when the Bank was put in operational charge of monetary policy.

Responsibility for borrowing was transferred to the UK Debt Management Office. In 2010 the Debt Office was having no trouble in managing the debt, which had an average maturity of some 14 years. The situation was far removed from that of Greece, whose government hardly knew whether it could rely on funds a mere few weeks ahead. But George Osborne stirred up a panic that the UK could be in the same position as Greece in what looked suspiciously like a politically motivated plan to introduce his strategy of austerity. And the Bank of England was very much to the fore in highlighting its concerns about the size of the deficit, even though the Debt Office was having no trouble in financing it.

Notes

1. 'Net trade' or 'exports minus imports'. Regular comments on the progress, or not, towards 'rebalancing' the economy in favour of exports have been made throughout George Osborne's chancellorship in the Bank of England's quarterly Inflation Report and the Office for Budget Responsibility's Economic and fiscal outlook.

CHAPTER 8

HOW TO DELAY A RECOVERY

Two IMPORTANT questions arise in relation to the reaction of the Treasury and the Bank of England to the new Chancellor's assessment of the economic situation in summer 2010. First, should the Bank of England, whose responsibility was for monetary policy and which had been granted independence in this area, have got itself involved in fiscal policy? Secondly, should the Treasury, which *is* responsible for fiscal policy, have taken such a narrow view of the crisis, and become so obsessed with the deficit, at the expense of concentration on economic growth?

The first question is almost rhetorical. Unelected central bankers should stick to their brief. The second question is more complicated. The Treasury, along with its successive Chancellors, had ridden with the boom and assumed that the revenue streams, from the City and elsewhere, to support higher public spending were more powerful and reliable than they turned out to be. Yet the Treasury knew full well that the incoming government was grossly exaggerating the degree to which the budgetary crisis was caused by Labour's (public spending) mess rather than the banking crisis. Indeed, as already noted, until the onset of the crisis, the public sector deficit as a proportion of gross domestic product had been lower than in most years under the Major government of 1992–97.

True, public spending had risen. But the only 'mess' that this increase was associated with was not riotous spending by Labour, but the impact of the financial crisis. Between 2008 and 2009, GDP, which in normal times had risen by an average of 2–2.5 per cent a year, plunged by 5.2 per cent and industrial production by 10 per cent.

In 2007, public spending as a share of GDP had, at 39.08 per cent, been broadly the same as under Kenneth Clarke's Chancellorship. The financial crisis was the factor behind a rise to 46.09 per cent in 2010 – the year that George Osborne became Chancellor. But in historical terms this was hardly a pretext for panic stations. In the last year of the Second World War (1945) public spending peaked at 70.34 per cent of GDP. And even during the build-up to the IMF crisis of 1976, from which the Callaghan government never recovered, the ratio of public spending to GDP did not rise above 48.28 per cent (in 1975). And there was no financial crisis in the mid-1970s, whatever the other problems with inflation and the unions.

Moreover, the economy was already 'on the mend' when Mr Osborne shouted 'fire'. As the National Institute Economic Review noted in October 2010, "The UK economy has now enjoyed four consecutive quarters of economic expansion". Indeed, GDP growth reached 1.2 per cent in the second quarter of that year, the fastest rate of growth in over a decade. This recovery had been supported by government spending, reflecting the 'stimulus' applied in 2009 when world trade was collapsing, and the Group of 20 had their historic meeting in London at the beginning of April 2009. But, as the National Institute for Economic and Social Research (NIESR) observed in October 2010, the economy now faced "weakness in demand due to both the household and public sectors simultaneously addressing the weakness of their balance sheets." This was the kind of 'balance sheet recession' diagnosed by Keynes in the 1920s and 1930s. But, as the NIESR pointed out, the expansion had been supported by government spending, and now "this positive contribution to GDP growth has probably stopped, given the impact of the cutback in government spending planned this year".

This analysis was published shortly after Ed Balls, not yet the Shadow Chancellor, had made a remarkably prophetic speech in August 2010 about the likely impact of Mr Osborne's austerity policies.

In the end, the Chancellor is in charge at the Treasury. In the words of one veteran official many years ago: "Governments do foolish things. My job is to see that they do foolish things properly." Officials can advise, but the Chancellor decides, with the Prime Minister, of course. Now, for many years after the war the Treasury was as interested in the management of demand in the economy as it was in the control of public spending. But, one way or another, the arrival of George Osborne in office appeared to coincide within the Treasury with a revival of the 'Treasury View' of the 1930s, against which John Maynard Keynes had railed for years.

True, the deficit inherited by the Coalition was large. But it had been much larger during previous crises, much larger. And this was most certainly a crisis. Alas, the Treasury seemed to forget its interest in demand management. There had been a huge reduction in output; there were fears about a marked rise in unemployment; and a recovery had just begun. It was worried about the budget deficit, but all experience showed that the best way of bringing a deficit down is for the economy to resume strong economic growth. There had been periods in the past when, as now, there were concerns about a so-called 'structural' deficit – that is, a deficiency in the nation's housekeeping that has nothing to do with the impact of recession, depression or the business cycle, and could prove lasting if action were not taken.

But there had also been times in the past when a 'structural' deficit had mysteriously disappeared after a period of rapid growth. The fact is that the distinction between a structural deficit and a cyclical one is difficult to draw. Nevertheless, even assuming that policymakers were right about the structural deficit, taking action to raise taxes and lower public spending was bound not only to stop the recovery in its tracks, but also to aggravate the underlying depression.

Indeed, with banks reluctant to lend there was a strong case for the government to step in and fill the gap. Keynes had demonstrated that in times of depression higher public spending was a sure way of alleviating the situation. At the time, and for some years to come, the government was able to borrow at negligible rates of interest, and could have done so on a large scale. Instead, the official forecasts actually showed a planned decline in public sector investment.

The collective decision of the policy machine was to accompany a fiscal squeeze with a monetary stimulus. But not only was a fiscal squeeze the last thing a fragile economy required: it was guaranteed to, and did, have a negative impact both on output and on the confidence of business and 'consumers'. As noted, the high priest of monetarism, Milton Friedman himself, had always maintained that monetary policy worked with 'long and variable lags'. (This was long before he recanted, in a celebrated interview in the *Financial Times*, on the very doctrine of monetarism with which he had been so closely associated.)

To recap: the Chancellor was conducting a policy of fiscal conservatism but monetary activism – or so he said. But fiscal contraction was not 'expansionary': there was a gaping hole in the economy – in what economists call 'aggregate demand' – and fiscal contraction was making it worse. Meanwhile, one did not have to be a monetarist to be concerned when, so far from expanding under a policy of 'monetary activism', the stocks of money and credit were in fact contracting.

It was this contraction that quantitative easing, or open market operations, was designed to offset. When the central bank wishes to shrink the money supply it sells securities to the banking system, thereby reducing the banks' base of cash and liquid assets, and therefore their ability to lend. When it wishes to expand the stock of money and the level of credit, it buys securities from the banks and puts money into the system, from which base banks can expand their lending.

For much of the 'flatlining' period, QE appeared to be more of a defensive operation, in practice, than one that was offsetting the contractionary effects of fiscal policy. Various explanations were readily given: banks were having to restore their capital base, indeed their solvency, and were so scarred by the experience of the crash that they were reluctant to lend. Alternatively, they were happy to lend but there was precious little demand for loans. To the extent that this second explanation was true – and there must have been quite a lot in it – it reflected the poor state of demand in the economy, and the prolonged depression of confidence and 'animal spirits'.

There is an old saying that 'you can lead a horse to water but you cannot force it to drink'. I am told by equestrian experts that the truth is even worse than that: that you cannot even lead a horse to water if it does not want to go.

However, a recovery did indeed begin, some three years after George Osborne's first deflationary budget. With a chutzpah that one has to admire, the Coalition has devoted itself to arguing that, because a recovery has at last begun, this justifies the policies and period of austerity that preceded it. Indeed, according to some versions of the Coalition's Newspeak, the period of austerity and planned penury for many was somehow the cause of the recovery.

The shamelessness of the Coalition and its supporters in a press that was largely hostile towards Labour knew few bounds. It became a common cry that the 'Keynesians' had been proved wrong because there were, finally, in 2013–14, the beginnings of a recovery. Worse, it was even alleged that the opposition to them was so twisted that we critics did not even want a recovery.

The truth is that of course we wanted a recovery. And I personally have no memory of ever maintaining that there would never be a recovery. Nor do I think other critics such as the redoubtable Martin Wolf and Sir Samuel Brittan of the *Financial Times*, or Lord Skidelsky held that odd position. The essential point was that, in a manner reminiscent of the Great Depression of 1929–31 and after, mistaken economic policies were delaying a recovery. The estimable Dave Ramsden, the Chief Economic Adviser to the Treasury – and I stress that advisers can only advise; they are not responsible for the policies of their political masters – would rightly maintain during those early days of the Coalition that '*economies GROW*'. The only question was when? And the fiscal stance, taking several percentage points off GDP every year, was inhibiting that recovery, with multiplier effects.

As noted, the 'multiplier' was an insight or invention of Richard Kahn's, the distinguished Cambridge economist who was a soulmate of Keynes's. Just as Keynes's essential insight was that, when you are in a hole you should stop digging, and take positive steps to get out, so Kahn's was that extra public spending – not 'cuts' but extra spending – could have multiplier effects, as the recipients of government contracts and hand-outs themselves went out to spend, multiplying the expansionary impact on demand.

The problem in the deflationary atmosphere of 2010 and after, both in the UK and eurozone, was, as the economists at the IMF belatedly realised, that the multiplier could operate in a negative direction, compounding the deleterious impact of the initial cuts.

One thing policymakers had learned from a study of the 1930s was that one should not add to the negative effects of a credit crunch by cutting the supply of money and credit even further. Hence, 'quantitative easing'.

Notes

1. Historical statistics for public spending come not only from the relatively modern Office for National Statistics but also from the old Central Statistical Office and its associated Economic Trends Annual Supplements.

2. Successive issues of the National Institute Economic Review have provided an invaluable commentary on the progress, or otherwise, of the Chancellor's deficit reduction strategy.

CHAPTER 9

ECONOMIES RECOVER
– EVENTUALLY

IF THERE WAS A SILVER LINING for the UK behind the clouds of unnecessary deflation, it was that things were not as bad here as in parts of the eurozone. As noted, Ed Balls, not at that stage appointed to the Opposition job for which he was most obviously qualified, gave a speech in August 2010, under the auspices of Bloomberg, in which he warned of a long period of stagnation unless Osborne changed the course of policy. He was right. But one limit to the deflationary scope of Osborne's strategy was a creation of Balls himself, for which the Coalition has never shown the gratitude it should. This was the fact that, under the terms of the legislation which gave the Bank of England operational control of monetary policy, the Monetary Policy Committee (MPC) was given a 'symmetrical' inflation target. That is to say, should inflation show signs of falling below 2 per cent per annum, the MPC was obliged to act to make monetary policy more expansionary. By contrast, until relatively recently, there had not been much sign of 'symmetry' in the European Central Bank's approach. Indeed, in spring 2014, the inflation outturn in the eurozone was well below its target of 'close to 2 per cent'; the danger of a descent into outright deflation has become more obvious; and, because the ECB's target is of course an average for all 18 member countries, outright deflation was becoming more of a threat in some countries outside Germany.

The classic textbook concern about deflation is that when prices are falling, people and businesses postpone purchases in the expectation that they will become even cheaper. Also, it was pretty firmly established after the Second World War that gently rising prices (on average), associated with a low inflation rate, were conducive to a general climate of expansion. The obvious example of an economy that has suffered from deflation after many prosperous decades is Japan, where it is a commonplace that the 1990s and the first 10 years of the present century were, as far as economic growth is concerned, 'two lost decades'.

So there is no doubt that the MPC itself, during the conduct of what George Osborne termed 'the long-term Plan' was biased in favour of expansion, insofar as it could offset the contractionary impact of the Coalition's deficit reduction strategy. The initial problem was the 'paradox of thrift' identified by Keynes when he advocated fiscal expansion as well as monetary stimulus to fend off depression. If everybody practices 'thrift', including the government, then demand remains depressed.

There are few things new under the sun, and there would have been nothing unfamiliar about quantitative easing to Keynes – other, that is, than the ugliness and arcane nature of the phrase itself.

But if there is nothing new under the sun, there are, from time to time, new insights which help to explain our relationship to the sun. While not, as it were, as earth-shattering as Copernicus's discovery that the earth rotated round the sun, and not vice versa, Keynes's *General Theory of Employment, Interest and Money* taught the world (one hoped!) that it did not make sense, when the private sector was suffering a depression, to aggravate the situation with cutbacks by the public sector.

Yet it has been a long haul for Keynesians. A very respected financial journalist wrote at the height, or depth, of the crisis words to the effect that: "When the private sector cuts back, then the public sector must also cut back." This is completely contrary to the Keynesian insight, which was a contribution of Copernican significance to the economics profession and to the wider political and diplomatic world.

However: although labelled a 'general' theory, the Keynesian analysis was particularly relevant to the specific situation of a collapse of output, employment and general confidence caused by a downturn in the business cycle associated with a banking crisis. I have studied over the years in libraries replete with learned volumes on 'business cycle theory', but the essence of business cycles is not difficult to grasp.

What tends to happen, as we have experienced once again in recent years, is that in boom conditions companies overexpand and individuals overspend; the financial markets accentuate the general feeling of what Alan Greenspan called 'irrational exuberance'; and, while some commentators argue that 'it will all end in tears' a kind of crowd mentality grips most people and we begin to hear what have been described as the most dangerous words in the English language: 'this time it's different' – i.e. the belief spreads that the business cycle has been abolished, and there will be no reaction or 'downswing'.

Gordon Brown made a crucial mistake which has haunted him ever since when he gave people the impression that 'boom and bust' had been abolished. This dreadful error was born in the heat of what at the time was a fine period for Brown in opposing the pre-1997 Conservative government. He made a party political point when promising 'no more TORY boom and bust'. The oracle of Delphi would have been content to utter that phrase, but the ambiguity was lost on the political class and the electorate in general. One has lost count of the number of times members of the public have cited that as a reason for their distrust of Gordon Brown who, as an accomplished historian, ought to have been well aware of the business cycle.

The problem for Keynesians, which most certainly proved useful ammunition to the austerity brigade of post-2009, was that, over the years, the essential message and relevant circumstances of Keynes's message had been distorted, indeed misinterpreted.

During the post-war years, policymakers were determined to avoid the kind of depression that afflicted the US, UK and wider world during the 1930s. Intense efforts were made to iron out the worst fluctuations of the business cycle. Thus the main aim of successive British budgets was to cool the atmosphere in boom conditions and take expansionary measures when unemployment was rising. It was accepted that inflation and the balance of overseas payments could often be a constraint on so-called 'Keynesian' measures. But the Keynesian currency was undoubtedly devalued in practice at times, often for crude electioneering reasons – and this gave scope for opponents of Keynesians to try to discredit the entire *oeuvre*.

Thus, during the recent years of austerity, the Osborne 'strategy' was upheld by its proponents on the grounds that Keynesian measures to expand the economy, or at least to limit the downturn, would somehow be 'inflationary'. Keynes himself had been as concerned about high inflation as most people, but high inflation, or even accelerating inflation from a low level, was not the problem in 2010–13.

The concerns about inflation were particularly linked to all that quantitative easing – 'printing money' being the permanent slogan of a certain type of critic. One is reminded of the joke that went the rounds during the early phases of monetarism in practice in Britain. Inflation was high, and the Thatcher government was repeatedly missing its 'monetary targets'. This gave rise to the remark 'sound money – and lots of it', which I first heard from Sir Samuel Brittan.

But the point about the QE, or open market operations, we have referred to above is that the entire exercise constituted an effort to offset a 'credit crunch' during which, so far from there being 'lots of it', both the money supply and the flow of credit had been contracting sharply. Moreover, there was another important aim: to try to supplement the decision to keep the Bank Rate at record lows with a policy of selling securities so that long-term rates could also be held down. In the bond market, when there is heavy buying of bonds this has the effect of reducing long-term interest rates; selling them has the reverse effect.

By 2013–14 the 'Great British Economic Recovery' was finally sighted and much lauded by the Chancellor, as if it justified all that had gone before – or, perhaps one should say, not gone before. Even the IMF, which had been critical of the Chancellor's policy, apologised for having suggested that with his deficit reduction strategy he had been 'playing with fire'. Strictly speaking, it was not the IMF itself, which has taken the practice of bureaucratic phrasing to a fine art, but its chief economist Olivier Blanchard, who had used the phrase in 2013 at a press conference.

Nevertheless, the IMF had been right to question this strategy. The fact is that it did hold up the recovery, and much damage was done. The beginnings of the 2013–14 recovery have taken place at a time when the UK's GDP is some 20 per cent below what it might have been expected to reach in accordance with historical trends. The recovery began partly because economies do eventually recover and partly because the enormous efforts put into monetary and credit expansion finally paid off. The danger is that they may have paid off almost too well.

Notes

1. Ed Balls, Bloomberg Speech. On 27 August 2010, when Shadow Secretary of State for Children and Education – in effect, Shadow Chancellor in Waiting – Ed Balls delivered a speech entitled: The case against the 'growth deniers' – how Labour can win the argument that there is an alternative.

   It was a powerful and prophetic speech, taking issue with George Osborne's entire strategy.

   He said that 'Against all the evidence, both contemporary and historical, he (Osborne) argues the private sector will somehow rush to fill the void left by government and consumer spending, and become the driver of jobs and growth.' Yes, there should eventually be a deficit reduction plan, 'but only once growth is fully secured and over a markedly long period than George Osborne is currently planning'. Evoking memories of that earlier period of austerity, Balls said: 'Just think if Clement Attlee's government at the end of the Second World War had decided that the first priority was to reduce the debts built up during the war – there would have been no money to fund the creation of the NHS, no money to rebuild the railways and housing destroyed in the Blitz, no moneys to fund the expansion of the welfare state."

2. A picture that television audiences became familiar with in the next few years was of Ed Balls, in the House of Commons, waving his arm horizontally towards the Chancellor, while uttering the word 'flat-lining!'

   It was too early for him to use this word two months after the election, but he did emphasise in his Bloomberg speech 'The data for the second quarter for GDP may have been strong [reflecting the earlier fiscal stimulus under Labour] but the signs are not encouraging for the second half of this

year' – when the early impact of George Osborne's deflationary budget would be felt.

PART III

AUSTERITY – THE OSBORNE EXPERIMENT

CHAPTER 10

AN OBSESSION WITH DEFICITS

EVERY AUGUST, when on holiday, I like to include one book on astronomy among those I take. The only 'Kindle' to interest me personally was the great economic historian Charles Kindleberger, who knew a thing or two about the causes and consequences of financial crashes.

Once the astronomers get on to astrophysics and string theory, they tend, as it were, to tie the reader, and sometimes themselves, in knots. Economists have a different kind of string theory, much more comprehensible: it is that using monetary policy to stimulate an economy can be compared to pushing on a string, at least in the early stages, when nothing much may happen. Later on, however, the appropriate metaphorical tool may be elastic, not least the elastic on a catapult. You pull it back; the missile remains stationary; and then, whoosh, it is hurled through the air.

Monetary policy in the UK during recent years seems to have begun with the economists' version of string theory and moved on, after a considerable time, to the catapult. The monetary weapon was eventually catapulted out of the sling; asset and property prices shot up; business surveys indicated much greater confidence; and more and more commentators and, indeed, participants in the financial world, began to make comparisons with the free-for-all that led up to the crash of 2007–08.

To change the metaphor yet again: I vividly recall a conversation with a senior Bank of England official in the dark days of 2008–09 who said: "We are going to have to throw everything at the economy, including the kitchen sink." That was in the first phase of the reaction, when officials were still feeling their way – realising that they had a bank insolvency crisis on their hands, as well as a mammoth liquidity problem. Those were also the days when, knowing how bad their own position was, nobody in the financial markets trusted anybody else, the great capitalist financial markets did not work, and world trade was collapsing at an annual rate of 20 per cent.

It was the 19th century British Chancellor and Prime Minister William Gladstone who once observed: "Finance is, as it were, the stomach of the country, from which all the other organs take their tone."

Gladstone himself was the high priest of the 'balanced budget' school of economic policy – an approach that used, frankly, to be laughed at by the economists advising on economic policy during the post-war years. The phrase 'Gladstonian finance' was a term of derision, used by people who regarded themselves as 'economically literate' against 'financial' commentators who had not absorbed the lessons of the Keynesian revolution.

These days there is an annual 'Wincott Award' in honour of the memory of Harold Wincott, a regular columnist on the *Financial Times* in the 1950s and 1960s. Yet, certainly in the late 1960s, most of the staff of the FT regarded Wincott's obsession with 'balancing the books' year by year, in Gladstonian fashion, as a bit of a joke. As the late Lord Croham, a distinguished Treasury Permanent Secretary, once commented: what mattered was balancing the economy, not the budget.

Britain has recorded a budget surplus in about a dozen years since 1945 – a period of almost 70 years. Indeed, a deficit to finance long-term capital expenditure was for many years regarded as normal and desirable. George Osborne's ambition not just to balance the books but to run a budget surplus by 2018 was first announced at the Conservative Party's annual conference in October 2013, and reiterated in his March 2014 Budget.

As it became clear in spring 2014 that there was most certainly an economic recovery under way in Britain, Osborne made a major speech to the right-wing American Enterprise Institute in Washington, at the time of the spring meetings of the World Bank and the IMF. He launched a frontal attack on his critics, arguing that the recovery had resulted from "an effectively deployed" monetary policy and "a credible fiscal policy".

It was certainly credible that Osborne was relying on a restrictive fiscal policy as one key element in his strategy, the other being, of course, the monetary policy deployed by the Bank of England.

As we have seen, there was an accumulation of measures: low interest rates (Bank Rate was kept at one half of 1 per cent. By contrast, during those post-war years of austerity 2 per cent was considered low enough); quantitative easing; assorted micro-schemes to encourage a greater flow of finance towards house purchase, and to augment the resources of small and medium-sized firms. Above all, however, what the economy required on the monetary side was a reconstituted banking system and a revival of confidence so that manufacturing and service companies would regain their 'animal spirits' and unveil new plans for investment and expansion. To do this, they needed the finance that Gladstone had described as "the stomach of the country".

A crucial point about the 2007–08 crash and its aftermath was that not one but several generations of politicians, officials, businessmen, bankers and economists had simply taken that financial stomach for granted. There had been business cycles since 1945, and several recessions, not least those associated with the two oil shocks of the 1970s; there had been the much discussed 'dotcom boom and crash' around the turn of the 20th and 21st centuries; and there had been the odd banking failure. But the banking and financial systems had not ground to a halt in the way they did in 2007–08. A few economic historians were aware of the banking crises of the 19th century, in 1914 and 1929–31; but somehow they had been assumed out of existence, or at least recurrence. Moreover, in Britain there was even less awareness of banking crises: it was a notable difference between the experience of the Depression in 1929–31 that the US underwent a banking crisis, as did some Continental countries, such as Austria. But in the UK there was no banking crisis.

It helped in the worldwide reaction to this latest crisis that the most influential central banker at the most important central bank, namely Ben Bernanke, had studied the Great Depression and drawn appropriate conclusions.

For British economic policymakers in mid-2010 there ought to have been a very obvious lesson of history: that lesson was that policymakers should not become obsessed with one economic indicator or objective, to the virtual exclusion of most others. Yet this is precisely what happened: the economy was beginning to recover from the worst recession since the Second World War, but was still seriously depressed. What was the one indicator that the new government focused on? It was the budget deficit, or the level of public sector borrowing. As noted, the average maturity on existing debt was 14 years, and the Debt Office was having no difficulty whatsoever in financing it. True, the figure could be made to look large – it was. But the more an economy grows, the larger at any one time will be the level of spending, and borrowing, in both the public and private sectors. As a proportion of GDP the deficit had been much larger, many times, in the past. The confidence of both business and its customers had collapsed, as had output, and there were severe concerns about the trend of unemployment. Moreover, if anything, the deficit that should have been causing most concern was not the budget deficit that one would expect to occur in the face of recession, but the deficit in the balance of payments, and especially in overseas trade.

This latter reflected the accumulation of a number of problems over the years, usually associated with misconceived policy decisions. Thus during the Thatcher period from 1979 onwards there had been a woeful neglect of manufacturing; manufacturing might have accounted for a declining proportion of GDP over the years, but it still contributed over half our export earnings. James Prior and Michael Heseltine, two of Mrs Thatcher's Cabinet Ministers at the time, subsequently revealed in their memoirs their astonishment about the way their colleagues neglected manufacturing and seemed to believe that the British economy could, in the future, rely entirely on the growth of income from 'services'. For many years this enfeebled trading position was masked by reliance on the flow of oil and gas from the North Sea. Any visitor from outer space looking at the British economy from a strategic point of view in mid-2010 would surely have been as concerned about the trade gap as about the deficit caused by the banking crisis.

All experience indicated that the best way to 'solve' a budget deficit problem was to grow out of it. But growth was evidently not the priority of the Coalition, or its members would have recognised that the surest way of restricting growth was to announce an austerity programme and quite deliberately raise taxes and cut public spending.

Over the years, successive arrays of British economic policymakers had indulged their obsessions. In the early 1980s the obsession with 'free markets' led the Thatcher government to tolerate a rise in the value of the pound to such absurd heights that British industry's competitive position in international markets was seriously damaged – so much so that the Chairman of what was then our leading chemical company, ICI, went to Number 10 to ask the Prime Minister if she wanted the company to survive and remain in Britain.

During that same period the government was also convinced that all the British economy's traditional problems with inflation would be solved if it could control the money supply. That effort fell victim to Goodhart's Law – once regulators try to control an economic variable, its relationship to other indicators changes: this law is widely credited to the British monetary economist Charles Goodhart, based on his experience at the Bank of England at a time during the late 1970s and early 1980s when monetarism was fashionable. As it turns out, the observation was first made by the Cambridge economist Lord Kaldor. The next obsession became membership of the European exchange rate mechanism, the ERM – again, as a means of controlling inflation. When that adventure ended in humiliating circumstances on Black Wednesday, 16th September 1992, the new chimerical panacea became 'inflation targeting'. Alas, success, up to a point, with that exercise – in keeping the consumer price index close to a low target rate – was accompanied by neglect of what was going on in the financial markets generally, and of the implications and consequences of 'financial engineering'.

Of course, under George Osborne the next obsession was the budget deficit. I am not suggesting that everyone who takes a different view from other critics and me is obsessed with the idea of a smaller state. There are many people, including government and Bank officials, who do not have a right-wing agenda but worry about deficits and borrowing. But it has become more and more obvious, in speeches and remarks made by every senior Conservative politician from David Cameron and George Osborne to Boris Johnson, that behind their crusade to cut the deficit lies another agenda: that is to reduce the size of the state itself, and in particular the social services and the welfare budget, in order to cut taxes. In other words, one is left with a growing suspicion that 'welfare recipients' are being blamed for a budgetary crisis that was caused largely by the temporary failure of the financial system, and the poor and the vulnerable are in practice being punished so that taxes can be reduced for the better off – not solely to reduce the deficit.

Notes

1. The quotation from Gladstone appears in the 1992 edition of the invaluable Oxford Dictionary of Quotations. It is from his Article on finance, 1858. It was unearthed by H.C.G. Matthew, in Gladstone 1809-1874, published in 1986. Until the financial crash of 2007-08, entire generations of economists and policymakers seemed to take a functioning banking system for granted. Something certainly went wrong with the stomach of this country, and many others, after the financial crash, and the 'tone' of the 'other organs' was indeed affected.

2. On taxation, it seemed to me the height, or depth of insensitivity for Chancellor Osborne to lower the top rate of tax from 50 per cent to 45 per cent in the midst of his deficit reduction programme. Again, in his Margaret Thatcher Lecture (28 November 2013) entitled What would Maggie do Today? The mayor of London, Boris Johnson, came out with that favourite right wing assertion that cutting higher tax rates actually increases revenue – he said that in 1979 the top 1 per cent of income earners accounted for 11 per cent of total income tax revenue, but by 2013 it was 30 per cent. This conveniently omits the point that there has been a gargantuan widening in what economists call 'the distribution of income', so that the upper echelons pay a lot more in income tax because they pay themselves a lot more.

CHAPTER 11

A CRISIS AGGRAVATED BY
HOUSING SHORTAGES

THE SPEECH given by George Osborne to the American
Enterprise Institute in April 2014 was one that he took more
seriously than some. It went through several drafts, and was
closely checked by the Prime Minister in advance. Osborne
saw the occasion as a golden opportunity to hit back at his critics, at a time when things were looking much better for him
politically – his 'omnishambles' Budget a year earlier had been
considered a disaster even by his close colleagues. Now he
could boast of a revival of economic growth, with forecasts of
more to come.

According to the Osbornian doctrine, this growth was the
consequence of his enlightened policies of deficit reduction
and firm fiscal foundations. Osborne has an arrogant streak to
his character, as well as an insensitive one. He was happy to be
fawning to the point of being oleaginous in his several references to the American 'right'; but he could not resist having a
go at his American critics on the left

Critics such as his 'friend' the Harvard economist and
former US Treasury Secretary Lawrence Summers were wrong
to argue that growth depended on endless budget deficits.
Here he was, getting the budget deficit down in the UK and
presiding over an economic revival. He gave no thought to

how, notwithstanding the planned reduction in the deficit, the economy might have performed during the early stages of the crisis if it had not been for the 11 per cent deficit (in relation to GDP) that he inherited in 2010. The truth is that such a deficit had been necessary to prevent the entire economic ship going under. Moreover, even the most diehard Keynesians do not advocate budget deficits for the sake of it.

The point that united his critics on both sides of the Atlantic was not that you could not have growth without massive deficits stretching into the future, but that the austerity programme was first delaying the recovery and then restricting its progress. Where Osborne may well have been on firmer ground – and only time will tell – was in taking on 'the pessimists' who were arguing that the advanced world might have entered a period of 'secular stagnation'. Such pessimism went back to the days of Thomas Malthus, he pointed out; and in the 1930s the US economist Alvin Hansen had predicted a long period of stagnation, but the US economy was now 13 times larger than when he made his prediction. This, incidentally, was a point he had taken from a speech made by Mark Carney to the New York Economic Club in December 2013.

The so-called 'secular stagnation' thesis, or its revival, is based on the empirical observation that each recovery in the past two decades or so, both in the US and UK, has been less impressive than in previous decades, and has arguably required ever greater monetary stimulus. But, as the American economist Paul Krugman has repeatedly pointed out, the latest recovery would almost certainly have been stronger if there had indeed been greater fiscal stimulus.

Osborne was having a go not just at the 'secular stagnation' school, but at all those who criticised his debt reduction programme. In particular, he had in mind the Chief Economist of the IMF at the time, Olivier Blanchard, who had argued that that, by rejecting a 'Plan B', the Chancellor had been playing with fire.

Yet, to a certain – quite large – extent he had been playing with fire. His policies during the first three years of his
Chancellorship aggravated and prolonged a recession caused
by the banking crisis. It was a relief when recovery was sighted.
But the IMF in spring 2014 echoed many critics on this side
of the Atlantic in drawing attention to the unbalanced nature
of the British recovery, with its dependence on yet more
consumer debt and the 'wealth effect' from higher property
prices. The latter had risen by 18 per cent in London in one
year, and it was widely reported by political correspondents
that the Chancellor had told his Cabinet colleagues that he
would woo the electorate with "a little property boom".

By mid-2014 house prices were rising at 12 per cent in the
UK as a whole and 20 per cent in London, so the boom was not
so little. There were a number of factors at work, the principal
one being the low rate of new house building over decades,
with developers 'sitting' on sites where they had planning
permission but were waiting for prices to rise further. Indeed,
the planning problem seemed to embrace two obstacles: the
difficulty of obtaining planning permission in the first place,
compounded by the hoarding issue. In London, the housing crisis was aggravated by the way the capital had become
a millionaire's, indeed billionaire's, investment opportunity,
often with buyers paying in cash, a phenomenon over which
Mark Carney said his 'prudential' weapons had no control.
The housing bubble has almost certainly been blown larger by
the favourable tax treatment of owner occupation, and the fact
that there has been no increase in rateable values since 1992.

Debates had been raging for years as to whether the manifest shortage of housing should be mitigated by developing
the 'green belt' or 'brownfield sites'. The underlying problem
was a severe shortage of supply. Successive governments had
neglected to fill the gap left in the availability of social housing
after the Thatcher government introduced its popular 'right to
buy' scheme (council properties) in the early 1980s. A 'prop-

erty owning democracy' had been a favourite slogan of the Conservatives since Anthony Eden popularised it in the 1950s. Home ownership for those who desire it seems a laudable aim, and the Callaghan government had flirted with the idea of selling council dwellings in the late 1970s, although nothing came of it. But there is always going to be a 'rented sector'.

Renting suits some people but is often a step on the ladder to home ownership. Unfortunately, the dearth of properties had contributed to often penal increases in rents, which were absorbing an unhealthily large proportion of the incomes of the poor.

It is indeed a commonplace that government policy towards the rented sector has become a mess. Right-wing tabloids complain about the size of the bills for housing benefit, but it is well established that exorbitant sums of housing benefit accrue to unscrupulous landlords. Attempts by the Coalition to control or reduce housing subsidies via what became known as the 'bedroom tax' turned out to be a very nasty exercise in social engineering. At one extreme, the poor have been urged, or forced, to move if they have a spare bedroom. At the other extreme, London is replete with large houses and apartments owned by rich foreigners – dwellings which contain many bedrooms that remain empty for most of the year. Meanwhile, East London councils have waiting lists of more than 10,000. Since the policy of austerity was put in place in 2010, the local newspapers have recorded many an instance of families – often with only one parent – having to move great distances into cheaper accommodation and in a way that disrupts the children's education and their relationships with relations and friends. One rationalisation is that these families are replaced by more urgent cases, but if the housing crisis had not been allowed to develop, such disruptive 'divide and rule' measures would not have been thought necessary.

This brings us to the nub of the phenomenon that distinguishes austerity now, in the UK, from austerity in the immediate post-war years, and austerity in parts of the eurozone.

Austerity in 1945–51 was experienced by most of the people, with even the young Princess Elizabeth and Prince Philip having to use clothing coupons for their wedding. Austerity in Greece has provoked riots and the rise of dangerous neo-fascist groups. By contrast, although average incomes in the UK have fallen in recent years and are only just beginning to recover, there has been precious little social disruption. The worst effects – reductions in state 'benefits' and maladministration in the distribution of 'entitlements' – have been causing hardship and misery to the 'voiceless'. Many of these have turned up on the doorsteps of the nation's churches. This is why those who can represent them with a voice, for instance the Archbishop of Canterbury and the Catholic Cardinal Archbishop of Westminster, have felt the need to speak out.

Notes

1. Re Chancellor Osborne's claim to the American Enterprise Institute that recent growth had been the consequence of his deficit reduction strategy: in March 2013, when growth was still depressed, prime minister David Cameron said that the OBR "are absolutely clear that the deficit reduction plan is not responsible". The OBR's director Robert Chote quickly responded: 'Every forecast published by the OBR since the June 2010 Budget has incorporated the widely held assumption that tax increases and spending cuts reduce economic growth in the short term.'

    (Martin Wolf FT 13 March 2013, in an article Britain's austerity is indefensible.)

2. The 11 per cent Budget deficit inherited in 2010 was almost entirely the consequence of the impact of the depression on

public spending and tax revenue. In Budget 2009 – Building Britain's future, subtitled Economic and Fiscal Strategy Report and Financial Statement and Budget Report, the Treasury calculated that the budget deficit in 2007–08 was 0.4 per cent. Even the so-called 'cyclically-adjusted' deficit was a mere 0.7 per cent of GDP. These figures could by no possible criterion justify the Coalition's jibe about inheriting 'Labour's mess.'

3. The following is an extract from Carney's speech, The Spirit of the season, to The Economic Club of New York, 9 December 2013, four months before Chancellor Osborne's address in Washington to the American Enterprise Institute: 'So while it is unsurprising that the ideas behind secular stagnation are being revived, it would be a mistake to rush to a more extreme macroeconomic response. There is a long history of pessimism in economics, from Thomas Malthus through Alvin Hansen to Robert Gordon. Such worries have proven misplaced in the past and scepticism is warranted now. Don't forget that he US economy is more than 13 times larger than when Hansen first formulated his ideas.'

CHAPTER 12

WHAT ABOUT THE WORKERS?

IN SPRING 2014 the Coalition was almost four-fifths of the way through its five-year term. Yet it had been only recently that the government had woken up to the two outstanding problems facing macroeconomic policy. One was the housing crisis, as earlier noted. The other was the trend of the balance of overseas payments: in the fourth quarter of 2013 the current balance of payments deficit was recorded at an annual rate of 5 per cent of GDP – not quite in the same league as the horrific situation facing the post-war Attlee government, but nonetheless larger than the kind of deficit that had provoked sterling crises and resort to borrowing from the IMF in the 1960s and 1970s.

The housing crisis was closely linked to monetary policy. Low interest rates and various government and Bank of England lending schemes had revived the demand for houses and were pushing prices up fast. One should never forget that most basic of economic concepts: the law of supply and demand. When demand rises in most spheres of the economy, that should conduce an increase in supply. There is bound to be a time lag, but in the housing market that lag can be very long indeed, given planning constraints, 'Nimbyism', and other obstacles referred to earlier. Meanwhile, the 'wealth effect' experienced by the beneficiaries of rising house prices boosts their contribution to the perceived recovery in consumer spending, while the burden of rising housing costs continues to be a drag on the real incomes of the poor.

The housing crisis and the negative trend of the balance of payments are closely related to the thinking behind that vogue phrase increasingly used by everyone from the Chancellor to the Chief Economist of the IMF, including successive Governors of the Bank of England: the 'need to rebalance the economy'.

Whereas the budget deficit problem to which the Coalition has devoted so much attention can be alleviated, if not entirely resolved, by a reasonable period of economic growth, the balance of payments deficit might well be aggravated. What is so remarkable about the payments deficit is that it has occurred during a period when the economy has been depressed. In the past, such gaps have appeared after a period of rapid growth.

A rebalanced economy would be exporting more, and relying less on imports. This would not mean that imports would be reduced, but that their growth, in relation to exports, would slow down. A stronger exporting sector implies the need for more business investment. In this context, after all the flatlining, there was a recovery in business investment in the course of 2013 and 2014 – a recovery which prompted the Chancellor to make a somewhat injudicious boast to his American audience in April 2014 that the UK was doing much better than the US in this respect.

But another aspect of rebalancing must surely be to arrive at a position where spending by consumers is less dependent on borrowing and rising house prices, and more the result of increases in real incomes. In the end, a nation's spending power is of course related to its productivity. One of the big talking points in the past year or two has been the relative stagnation of productivity, usually defined as 'output per person employed'.

The long-term tendency has been for productivity in the UK to rise by around two to 2.5 per cent a year. Indeed, it is estimated that if the historical trend had continued, output in the UK would be some 20 per cent higher in 2014 than it is expected to be. Obviously, that trend was disturbed by the onset of the crisis, but the gravamen of the case against Mr Osborne's policies of austerity, and their concomitant effect on confidence, is that the damaging impact of the crisis was substantially aggravated.

It was clear that the 'stimulus' of 2009 had stopped the rot; the problem was the premature withdrawal of that stimulus on the fiscal side, leaving monetary policy with too much to do. As the Office for Budget Responsibility (OBR) has pointed out, after 2008 there was a fall in average hours worked, and with it a reduction in real incomes; these, in 2014, were some 6 per cent below the position before the crisis. In the early Thatcher years there was a severe recession which led to a rise in unemployment to over 3 million. Given the horrors of the 2007–08 crisis and its immediate aftermath, many forecasters were expecting a similar experience. In fact, employers tended to hoard labour and instead of losing jobs, many people became 'part time' or were given what were known as 'zero hours' contracts. The figure for those in employment rose by 1 million between 2008 and 2014 but productivity stagnated. The increase in consumer spending when real incomes were flat was attributable not only to people drawing on savings or getting further into debt: there was also the impact of the increase in the labour force – "more people" as one labour economist succinctly put it.

There has been a certain insensitivity in the way Ministers, officials, and economists generally have referred to the trend of unemployment since the onset of the financial crisis. While, in human terms, it is surely a relief that 'the hit' has been taken by lower productivity rather than the huge increase in unemployment that many people expected, an unemployment figure of over 2 million is still nothing to shout about. As noted, there are frequent stories in the right-wing tabloids about 'scroungers' milking the social security system, and there is no doubt that such people do exist. Moreover, the balance between the level of benefits and available wages – the problem of 'incentives' and 'disincentives' – has been with governments throughout the western world for decades. But all the evidence shows that the workshy are a tiny minority, and that most people desperately want to work, and, of course, for a decent wage – often referred to as a 'living wage'. 'Living wages', in circumstances of low inflation, are likely to boost demand, morale and productivity.

The converse of the deeply unpleasant tabloid stories is the proliferation of reports in other national newspapers, as well as regional and local ones, about jobs for which hundreds of applicants apply, all but one of whom are inevitably doomed to be disappointed. Again, one's heart bleeds for the men and women, and indeed youths, who have just left school, when one reads of cases where they have applied for hundreds of jobs and been turned down every time.

When there is such a huge gap as there has been in recent years between the numbers of unemployed and the availability of jobs, it is blindingly obvious that there is a social problem which can only be resolved by an increase in economic activity and the accompanying demand. That is why the belated recovery is to be welcomed. Successive governments of both major political parties have toyed with all manner of what are known as 'active labour market policies' and we are always told that they are successful in places like Scandinavia and Wisconsin. But in the UK there seems to be a chronic difficulty with marginal tax rates, which are supposed to discourage people from taking jobs because it is not worth their while. There is certainly something unbalanced about government policies that aim at ever lower marginal tax rates for the rich, but penalise the poor with higher marginal rates.

To repeat: the workshy are a tiny minority, although, in one of the most reprehensible (of many) actions of the Thatcher government, there was a cynical policy of in effect encouraging

idleness. This occurred in the following way: as the unemployment figures rose from over 1 million to 1.5 million, 2 million,
2.5 million and 3 million, even the hard-line, 'dry' members
of Mrs Thatcher's Cabinet became embarrassed by the public
manifestation of what were in fact the consequences of their
own policies. What did they do? They proceeded from a state of
embarrassment to one of shamelessness, by quite deliberately
instructing civil servants to move many of the unemployed
from a position where they received unemployment benefit,
and therefore boosted the unemployment total, to one where
they received 'disability' benefit, and came off the unemployment roll. A government that had, in Opposition, campaigned
on the slogan 'Britain Isn't Working' – when unemployment
was 1.3 million – and professed to discourage 'welfare scroung-
ing' actually encouraged it, with longer-term consequences
about which the tabloids were able to bleat.

This sort of thing fostered the popular belief that there was
a kind of *non*-reserve army of 'unemployables'. But to anyone
who believes that 'unemployables' constitute a significant
proportion of the population, I commend a report in the old,
broadsheet *Wall Street Journal*, which one day contained a
fascinating story, based on research in Chicago, proclaiming
in the headline something like "Unemployables found to work
quite well..." And that was in a very right-wing newspaper.

There will always be 'frictional unemployment', when people
are 'between jobs'. And there is bound to be 'structural' unemployment when old industries die, or not-so-old firms relocate
production elsewhere. Then there is 'cyclical' unemployment,
when, as happened with a vengeance in recent years, there is
a downturn in the business cycle. 'Structural' unemployment
requires active regional policies on the part of the central
government, and dynamic action from regional authorities
to attract firms to the region and encourage local 'start-ups'.
One of the lessons of the 1945–51 period of austerity was that
regional policies could be very successful.

It was therefore a mercy that unemployment did not rise to quite the heights forecasters had expected; but an unemployment total of 2.3 million, or close to 7 per cent of the labour force, was still far too large for a civilised society, and the rapid reduction during 2014 may have taken the forecasters by surprise, but is most welcome. It is to the credit of Mark Carney that, from the moment he arrived at the Bank of England, he made a reduction in unemployment one of the key aspects of policy by which he would be judged. Indeed, he highlighted unemployment to such an extent that many commentators got the impression that other factors that must be weighed in policy decisions were being ignored – a lesson that Carney eventually learned, and to which he responded by emphasising the importance of other economic indicators too. (In fact, such factors had been there in the small print.)

It is interesting that, for all the hopes the great Maynard Keynes harboured that his generation's grandchildren would if anything be faced with 'the problem of leisure', unemployment, and indeed the achievement of a decent standard of living, still bulk so large in economic debate. In the end, the 'dismal science' of economics is meant to aim at satisfying people's needs and wants – the textbooks of my youth seemed to be preoccupied with the desirability of 'consumer satisfaction'. Then, of course, economists such as J K Galbraith in *The Affluent Society* and *American Capitalism* pointed out that there was an entire industry out there creating wants that people might otherwise not have thought of, not least via the discovery by car manufacturers and others of the profitable pastime – for them – of 'planned obsolescence'.

Most research seems to confirm the common-sense view that, although people may fantasise when on holiday about not going back to work, nevertheless there comes a time when, however much they may grumble, the return is considered not to be such a bad thing, if only because they need the money and like the routine. The main point about the large number of people in recent years who have been counted as 'employed', and about whose numbers George Osborne boasted in March 2014 when contriving to regard them as 'fully employed', is that most part-timers in recent years have been so not as a matter of choice. Clearly, if people choose to work part-time, that is fine with them. And there has certainly been a trend, not least among working married couple, or 'partners', for part-time work to become a matter of choice and convenience.

The minutes of successive deliberations of the Bank of England's Monetary Policy Committee (MPC) reveal that the Committee has been divided on just how to assess the extent of voluntary and involuntary unemployment and part-time employment. This has been an important question for some time, because the amount of 'slack' in the economy tradition-ally determines how much inflationary pressure there is, or is not, to worry policymakers. This assessment in turn affects decisions about interest rates. It ought, in my view, also to have an influence on fiscal policy. For many years policymakers did not rely simply on the monetary armoury in determining macroeconomic policy, but also on changes in public expend-iture plans and tax rates. This became unfashionable during the 1980s, partly because there was some evidence that time lags between the decision to increase public spending and the actual event could mean that the original purpose became out of date. As was typical of the British polity, there was an overre-action, so that all such measures were ruled out, and monetary policy assumed the central role. In the mid-1980s the former premier Sir Edward Heath compared Chancellor Lawson to "a one club golfer" for relying too much on interest rates.

It was an interesting change. As Sir George Blunden, then Deputy Governor of the Bank of England, once told a Commons Committee, the Bank of England had for years observed that changes in interest rates tended to take place primarily with an eye on the exchange rate – either to raise it or to lower it. Those were pre-independence days, when the Chancellor, and often the Prime Minister, decided when to alter rates, but always after taking advice from the Bank.

Reliance on monetary policy has been enormous. At the Conservative Party Conference in October 2013 the Chancellor continued to proclaim the need for a fiscal squeeze to reduce the deficit, with the aim of achieving a budget surplus before the end of the decade, irrespective, apparently, of the state of the economy. The month-to-month management of demand in the economy, given this background, is entirely in the hands of the MPC, and it has made assessments of how much 'spare capacity' there is in the economy into a central preoccupation. The OBR has been somewhat less optimistic than the economists Bill Martin and Professor Robert Rowthorn, who specialise in this area. Robert Chote, the Director of the OBR, summarised the position in April 2014 as being that, according to whom you listened, GDP could expand between 1 and 5 per cent before being hampered by capacity constraints.

The plot thickens. After almost three wasted years of flatlining, and the beginnings of a recovery in 2013, forecasts of economic growth in the UK were being revised upwards month by month, so that we reached the strange position in late April 2014 when the Confederation of British Industry was hailing the prospect of the best outlook for manufacturing for decades, with respect to orders for both the home market and export.

Commentators such as Larry Elliott of the *Guardian* were making comparisons with the spurt of growth in 1973, the years of the so-called 'Barber boom', when rates of 5 per cent (real) growth per annum were achieved, before it all ended in tears. The Barber boom was in reality the Heath boom: Heath was a strong Prime Minister with a 'hands-on' approach to the economy. Anthony Barber was a relatively weak Chancellor and, left to himself, would probably not have taken the brakes off the economy with such abandon.

There are interesting comparisons and differences with that period. Then, as more recently, the economy had been in recession. But in those days, political and social tolerance of high unemployment was much less than it is these days. An unemployment level of 1 million in the winter of 1972–73 had been enough to cause panic stations at Downing Street, and the emphasis of both monetary and fiscal policy became one of expansion, expansion, expansion, with an official target rate of growth of 5 per cent!

More recently the recession has been much deeper: indeed, as noted, I regard it as having been worthy of the description 'depression'. It is a theme of this book that, in contrast to 1972–73, fiscal policy has been contractionary, so that all the weight of 'recovery policy' has been placed on a mixture of easy money and exhortation, or what the Americans call 'jaw-boning'.

Here we come to an interesting test of the approach that Mark Carney brought to the party. He aimed at 'escape velocity' – rapid escape from recession. He made a big thing of 'forward guidance', betting his reputation on a promise that interest rates would remain low for a long time. This was taken by many as meaning for several years, right up to the May 2015 election. Yet more and more commentators were becoming uncomfortable with this commitment, and this is explored further in the next chapter.

Notes

1. George Osborne's 30 September 2013 speech at the Conservative Party Conference was intended to make a splash and did. There were the usual jibes about the 'inheritance', accompanied by the remarkable pronouncement on fiscal policy: 'We will aim to achieve an absolute surplus in the next Parliament, provided the recovery is sustained.'

    True, the word 'provided' implied that he would not be so pre-Keynesian as to aim at an 'absolute' surplus during a recession. But the key point was that, with the word 'absolute' he was committing a future Conservative government to aiming at a surplus on both current AND capital account during normal times, something which does not accord with the sensible convention that borrowing for long term investment should be treated separately.

The suspicion that cuts in the public services are to a considerable extent ideologically inspired, rather than a necessary reaction to the financial crisis, was strengthened by his assertion in the same speech: 'only if we properly control public expenditure will we be able to keep lowering taxes for hardworking people in a way that lasts.'

I read the word 'control' here as a euphemism for 'cut'.

2. Capacity constraints: the important paper on this subject by Bill Martin and Robert Rowthorn, 'Is the British economy supply constrained? II' was published in May 2012 by the Centre for Business Research, University of Cambridge. The Bank of England went into the issue in its February 2014 Inflation Report, as did the Office for Budget Responsibility in its March 2014 Economic and fiscal outlook.

CHAPTER 13

THE IMPORTANCE OF THE
EXCHANGE RATE

IN ONE OF my *Observer* columns early in 2014 I coined the term 'forward misguidance'. I was only half-joking. It may well turn out that, like Marx's quip about capitalism, Carney's term 'forward guidance' contained the seeds of its own destruction. By this I mean in the sense that, by emphasising that he intended to keep interest rates at rock bottom for a very long time – at one stage analysts were interpreting this as implying right up to the next election, in May 2015 – Carney might have unleashed forces which would drive rates up well before then. Indeed, by mid-2014, as Carney's statements about likely developments in interest rates began to chop and change, the appropriate phrase seemed to be 'backward guidance'.

It was interesting that the Governor began to cover his back by referring to the 'normalisation' of interest rates in due course, and implied that 3 per cent or so might be a ceiling. This would compare with a Bank rate of 5 per cent to 5.75 per cent in 2007, just before the financial crisis. Even such a relatively low ceiling, by comparison with the kind of rates experienced during the inflationary days of the 1970s and 1980s, would cause distress to borrowers who had overcommitted themselves at much lower rates. Their public statements indicated that Carney and his colleagues were all too aware of this.

In the low inflation days of the 1950s the 'panic' figure for Bank Rate was 7 per cent. That was usually when sterling was under pressure and incentives had to be offered to money managers to keep their funds in London. But after falling by almost 30 per cent between early 2007 and 2009, the (weighted average) exchange rate of the pound against other currencies recovered about a third of this loss between 2013 and the first half of 2014 – something that began to worry the Monetary Policy Committee because of the effects on competitiveness.

Thus during the closing stages of Mr Osborne's 2010–15 economic experiment, a conflict seemed to be arising between the possible need to raise interest rates to control the house price boom, and the need to avoid a rise that would, other things being equal, be expected to make placing funds in London more attractive, and thereby render the pound even less competitive.

I say 'other things being equal' because there could easily be a reaction the other way, if the world's financial markets suddenly, or for that matter gradually, became concerned about the trend of our balance of overseas payments, and there were to be an old-fashioned 'run on sterling'.

Of course, the other factor militating against a rise in interest rates was fear that the longed-for recovery might be arrested in its tracks. Here we come to what might well turn out to have been a strategic mistake on the part of a Chancellor who appeared in the first half of 2014 to 'have got away with it'. Even observers who were not so gullible as to swallow the Chancellorial whopper that the recovery was caused by, or necessarily followed, the period of flatlining – even those observers were beginning to think that Chancellor Osborne had pulled it off.

Essential to the Chancellor's case was that the fiscal squeeze had been a necessary condition for the recovery. But what seemed to be emerging in the course of 2014 was evidence that, by placing all his cards on the monetary table, Osborne had seriously unbalanced a policy that was intended to rebalance the economy.

In macroeconomic management, Chancellors have three principal tools of policy: fiscal policy; monetary policy; and exchange rate policy. The latter is closely linked to monetary policy – changes in interest rates affect the level of sterling – but is still worth thinking of as a separate category. However, before coming to what I regard as the imbalance in Osborne's fiscal and monetary policies, we need a brief diversion on exchange rate policy.

For many years, in the course of my work, I used to visit successive Governors of the Bundesbank, the German central bank. Whenever the subject of exchange rate policy came up in the UK, and commentators such as me would complain, as we often did, that the pound was overvalued, a frequent riposte was: "But look at Germany. The German economy is the envy of the rest of Europe, indeed the rest of the world, and the Germans do not need these devaluations".

Well, one of the reasons why they did not need devaluations was that their productivity was better than ours and their levels of inflation were much lower – so much so that at a crucial stage in his Chancellorship (1983–89) Nigel Lawson decided to 'shadow the D-mark' (in policy towards the sterling exchange rate) in the hope that Britain could bask in the Germany economy's shadow and somehow conquer inflation.

But the idea that German economic policymakers deliberately pursued a high exchange rate policy is plain wrong. On several occasions when I visited Karl Otto Pöhl, then President of the Bundesbank, in the 1980s, we would have very frank à deux conversations about exchange rates, and he always had a table of comparative real exchange rates close to hand. The Germans may have had many better economic practices than the British, but they were always aware of the need to prevent the D-mark from rising too high. Indeed, a frank admission by the then State Secretary at the Finance Ministry in the late 1970s to Chancellor Denis Healey about one of Germany's motives for joining the exchange rate mechanism was, according to Healey in his memoirs, a decisive factor behind his opposition to putting the pound into that mechanism.

Once again, in the course of the Osborne Chancellorship, one finds commentators arguing that the exchange rate no longer matters. This is partly to rationalise the partial reversal of the 2007–09 devaluation, and partly because they draw the conclusion from the trend of the trade balance that devaluation no longer works.

There are several points to be made here. One is that, in the absence of that devaluation, the current account of the balance of payments would almost certainly have deteriorated even further. In any case, as the Office for Budget Responsibility has pointed out, the devaluation did indeed assist the trend of the visible or merchandise trade balance.

Again, over previous decades, under both Conservative and Labour governments – and especially during the early Thatcher 'sado-monetarist' experiment – the manufacturing base was progressively eroded. An appropriate exchange rate would alter the balance, but these things take time – a long time. Under Cameron and Osborne, the present government has been paying lip service to the importance of the manufacturing sector. But one fears that, in the run-up to the 2015 election, and with real incomes having been squeezed for so long, there may be a cynical political motive in the toleration of the 'recovery' in the pound, because of the effect it has in temporarily making imports cheaper and therefore boosting the public's purchasing power.

Back for a second to Germany: most commentators are quick to point out that the policies of 'austerity' in Spain, Italy, Portugal and, especially, Greece, have been far more severe than in the UK. Here we come to an important background factor to the setting-up of the eurozone, and its consequences.

As is well known, the motive force behind the formation of the European Union itself and, later, the eurozone, was political: bringing together a Continent that had been ravaged by periodic wars for centuries, and, in particular, uniting France and Germany sufficiently so that war between those two would be unthinkable. (Germany had invaded France three times between 1870 and 1940!)

However, the Bundesbank, which had been celebrated for its success in keeping inflation under control for decades, prized its independence, and was far from keen initially on the eurozone. It fought hard to make the new European Central Bank even more independent of political interference than itself. But, and here we are back to exchange rates, given what became an unavoidable historical force, both the Bundesbank and the German Finance Ministry saw a golden opportunity to end the cycle of other European economies, most notably Italy, periodically devaluing against the German currency. The consequences have been seen in recent years: there can be little doubt that part of Germany's relative economic success during the aftermath of the financial crisis and the recent austerity has been due to its competitive exchange rate vis-à-vis the others – an exchange rate which was 'locked in' by the formation of the eurozone; conversely, part of the competitiveness problem facing Italy has been its inability, under the very structure of the single currency arrangements, to adjust its currency against that of Germany.

An appropriate exchange rate is therefore crucial to the smooth functioning of an economy. One of the great, albeit negative, achievements of Gordon Brown's Chancellorship was his resistance to any idea that the UK should lose the flexibility of the exchange rate. The performance of the British economy during the 'flatlining' years would almost certainly have been even worse if we had been locked into the eurozone. But the partial loss of the gain to competitiveness in 2007–09 is calculated to aggravate the underlying problem with the balance of payments. As noted, however, the short-term 'benefit' of cheaper imports is likely to help a Coalition that for a time has been faced with Labour's concentration on the squeeze on living standards.

Notes

1. Governor Carney: The reader will have gathered that I have mixed views about his governorship so far. There are conspiracy theorists who think his more dovish pronouncements about interest rates are evidence of some secret deal with the Chancellor who went to such great lengths to hire him. But they can be explained by his genuine concern about the dangers of premature action to stall the recovery and damage many overextended households. Also, the confusion stemming from some of his pronouncements no doubt reflects the confusion within the MPC itself, where the hawks were becoming increasingly vociferous.

   Despite his emphasis on macro- prudential tools of policy – which include the various attempts to control the house price boom without raising interest rates – he is nevertheless on record as saying that, while macro prudential policy 'affects the economic cycle, it is not suited to managing it. Instead its effects on the economic cycle should – like fiscal policy – be taken into account in setting monetary policy, which is the primary and most effective tool of demand management.' (Mais Lecture: One Mission. One Bank. Promoting the good of the people of the United Kingdom, Cass Business School, City University, 18th March, 2014.)

   Governor Carney's concern about unemployment and the impact of social inequality on growth were manifested in a lecture 'Inclusive capitalism: creating a sense of the systemic' at the Financial Times conference on Inclusive Capitalism, London, 27 May 2014.

I was particularly struck by something he said in an interview I did with him for the TUC 2014 Conference handbook: 'You know, we can call it wasteful spare capacity but, really, we're talking about people who want to work that can't find work because the economy is too weak.' (13 August 2013).

2. The exchange rate: the importance of the exchange rate has been central to British economic policy throughout the half century during which I have been involved in financial journalism.

John Mills, of the Exchange Rate Reform Group, is a tireless campaigner for a 'more competitive and realistic exchange rate.' He has recently, under the auspices of Civitas, written two lively pamphlets on the subject: *A Price That Matters – Britain's disastrous exchange rate policy'* (April 2012) and *There Is An Alternative – An economic strategy for 2015* (March 2014).

CHAPTER 14

KEYNESIANS VERSUS THE REST

GEORGE OSBORNE has been a very political Chancellor. I always suspected that, even though his deficit reduction strategy was debatable, and the forecasts had continually to be revised, this was of little consequence to him. He had his eyes on the 2015 election, whose fixed date had been his idea during the Coalition negotiations in 2010. His basic strategy was 'to get the pain out of the way' and then appeal to the electorate on the grounds that it had all been worth it, indeed necessary for the eventual recovery. For it was highly unlikely that there would not be a recovery at some stage, if for no other reason than that businesses have to replace and update equipment.

Although some of his advisers tried to restrain him, the Chancellor could hardly conceal his glee as 2014 progressed, the pace of recovery accelerated, and the rising pound made imports cheaper, thus boosting purchasing power. The recovery in the pound was unlikely to last, but he could gamble that the reckoning day, when the financial markets would finally wake up to the underlying instability of the UK's overseas trading position, could well be after the election. Meanwhile, as noted, the Bank of England might be becoming increasingly concerned about the bubble in house prices, but Osborne had reportedly boasted to his Cabinet colleagues that the electorate would enjoy a good old-fashioned house price boom.

Not all of them would, by a long chalk. The difficulties for the younger generation in finding 'affordable' housing were becoming a major talking point. And as noted, given Britain's chronic shortage of housing, tenants were finding the level of rents a great burden. Just as the balance of payments problem had been developing over a number of years, under successive governments, so had the housing crisis. The Labour Party began in May 2014 to flirt with the idea of rent controls, a suggestion that was immediately seized upon by 'market' economists, who emphasised that the real problem was a shortage of houses.

Here we come to an interesting aspect of the differences between what extreme 'market' economists believe and what actually happens in reality. There are, manifestly, cases of unscrupulous landlords, not least those who have been milking the welfare system in a way that distorts the original purpose of well-intentioned policies designed to assist the poor tenant, not the rich landlord.

Thus, despite the near-universal consensus among my fellow economists, rent controls are not all bad, if aimed at counteracting exploitation of tenants. But they are not a permanent solution to the housing crisis. Indeed, the recent financial crash gave us a perfect example of the flaws in pure market economics. All over Europe, there were, and still are, surpluses of housing, as well as shortages. It is just that in real life most people cannot benefit from that surplus. Thus in the run-up to the crisis there were housing booms in Spain and Ireland. When the crash came, whole estates were left unoccupied. Meanwhile, in the UK successive governments had not paid enough attention to the housing shortage, which was of course aggravated by the increase in the population. In real life it was impossible for the market to 'clear' by encouraging people in the UK to move to empty houses in Spain or Ireland. That is not the way the world works.

The consequences of the housing shortage were therefore seen in the rapid rise in house prices. This began to worry more and more observers of the economic scene, not least on the Bank of England's monetary policy and financial policy committees. Mr Carney had made it plain that he favoured what are known as 'macro' and 'micro' prudential measures to deal with such a threat, before embarking on the traditional response of raising Bank Rate. Such measures included easing up on the extent of government schemes to help people via assistance with mortgages to purchase property, as well as tighter control of the terms on which lending for house purchase can take place. But my impression was that certain members of the Financial Policy Committee, whose brief it is to safeguard financial stability rather than manage interest rates, were beginning to regard these prudential tools as insufficient in themselves.

A stark example of the problem was provided by the situation in London, where housing experts calculated that there was an underlying demand for some 52,000 houses a year, but a supply of only half that number.

For critics such as me, it was beginning to look as though, while government and Bank were professing to rebalance the economy, what was increasingly required was a rebalancing of monetary and fiscal policy.

Because of the tightness of fiscal policy – the IMF reckoned it amounted to a cumulative 5 per cent of GDP from 2010 to 2014 – the entire weight of policy aimed at a recovery had fallen on monetary policy. In his speech to the American Enterprise Institute (AEI) in December 2013, George Osborne had stated: "The pace of our fiscal consolidation over the last four years has been steady, with an average annual reduction in the cyclically adjusted primary balance of around 1.6 per cent of GDP according to the IMF – the largest and most sustained of any major advanced economy." Yet interest rates could not remain at rock bottom indefinitely, and low interest rates were having the inevitable effect of driving up asset prices, not least, given the shortage of supply, the price of those important physical assets known as houses.

Another interesting aspect of economic developments in 2014 was that, while proclaiming the arrival of the long-awaited recovery – which was supposed to be the reward for the earlier austerity – George Osborne was promising more austerity with regard to the public finances for the future. The aim of achieving a budget surplus later in the decade was first announced at the Conservative Party Conference in October 2013 and repeated in the Budget of spring 2014. This surplus was evidently to be achieved in current and capital spending combined, whereas it had been generally accepted over the years that capital spending – 'investment' – was a long-term affair which could be financed by long-term borrowing and should be treated separately.

Furthermore, the 'right wing' nature of the deficit reduction strategy was becoming more open. Thus the Chancellor was now looking for a further 25 per cent reduction in the public services budget, and openly talking about shrinking the size of the state. Two interesting pieces of serious economic analysis, by the economists Professor Brian Henry and Michael Lloyd respectively, came to the same conclusion: in effect the Osborne strategy was not primarily about reducing the size of the budget deficit. It was about reducing the size of the state, and with a particular emphasis on cutting welfare spending. That is to say, the focus of 'austerity' was principally on the poor and the disadvantaged who were turning up at church doors, and having recourse to the proliferating food banks.

The government's bias against the public sector was borne out by the way that Osborne emphasised to the AEI that 80 per cent of the deficit reduction would be achieved "through spending cuts and entitlement reform". For many years it had been taken as a rule of thumb that any necessary budget cuts would be divided 50–50 between public spending and taxation.

This is a good moment to emphasise that those of us known, often derogatorily, I fear, as Keynesians do not advocate current budget deficits as some article of faith. Nor do we think the health of the economy depends on deficits in perpetuity. Keynes himself was very conscious of financing needs, the title of one of his most celebrated works being How to Pay for the War. There have been two essential differences between what one may categorise as 'The Keynesians' and 'The Rest' in recent years. First, the broad Keynesian approach can be epitomised by the epigram much used by former Labour Chancellor Denis Healey in the 1970s: "When you are in a hole, don't dig deeper." If the private sector is cutting back, it simply does not make sense for the public sector to do so as well, thereby accelerating the collapse in demand for goods and services. Yet prominent commentators in both the US and UK advocated just that approach when we were in the depths of the recent depression.

Unfortunately, the general public seems obsessed with the idea that 'household economics' should also apply to the nation. There are indeed times, as most readers must have experienced, when one has to cut back one's household expend-iture. But one person's spending is another person's income, as the Nobel prizewinner Paul Krugman has repeatedly tried to get across in his New York Times column. What happened in 2008–09 was a collapse in demand for goods and services throughout most of the Group of Seven nations: early calcula-tions were that in the US, GDP fell by 4.3 per cent between April 2008 and June 2009 and in the UK the reduction was as much as 7.2 per cent. This compares with average trend growth rates over the long term of 2 to 2.5 per cent. In the calendar year 2009, UK GDP was at first estimated to have fallen by 5.2 per cent. This was later revised by the Central Statistical Office in the summer of 2014 to 4.1 per cent. As the City economist Rob Wood commented after the revision: "The revisions do not change the big picture. The recession was still huge, even if it has now gone from perhaps 10 to 9.9 on the Richter Scale."

This was why the 2008–09 coordinated rescue operation was needed. Not to have introduced what became known as 'the stimulus' would have been economically suicidal. Mr Osborne was slow to grasp this point, and too quick to embark on withdrawing the stimulus when he came to office.

The second essential difference between The Keynesians and The Rest concerned the manner and timing of the hoped-for return to budgetary normality. What Keynesians regarded as premature cuts in public spending, or premature increases in taxation, would mean that policymakers were 'digging deeper' if the private sector was still depressed, and at the very least delaying the recovery when there were eventually signs of life in the private sector. There is a time and a place for fiscal tightening, and 2010 was not one of them.

It has been put to me that the austerity strategy was a form of insurance policy, presumably against attack from the financial markets. But the idea, as still being propagated by George Osborne in 2014, that Britain was almost bankrupt in 2010 never rang true. If anything the financial markets could not acquire enough British government securities. The situation was in no way comparable to that in 1945.

Although I believe that there has been a strong element of ideology behind Chancellor Osborne's emphasis on austerity, as well as a political calculation that may yet prove to work in his favour, I am well aware that there are plenty of examples of inefficiency in the public sector. Thus there can be little doubt that many supporters of the Coalition's strategy are not intent on shrinking the size of the state for the sake of it, but simply wish to make public services more efficient. This was, incidentally, one of the principal aims of the Blair government.

As I write, there are widespread concerns about productivity in the economy at large, but Robert Chote of the Office for Budget Responsibility has detected signs of improvement in the productivity of the public sector, after a long period when official measures showed no such progress. But this does not, to my mind, justify a strategy which delayed the recovery for so long, and has exacerbated social problems.

Notes

1. Brian Henry, a most rigorous professional economist, who has worked at the Bank of England and the National Institute of Economic and Social Research, wrote a devastating critique of Chancellor Osborne's approach in 'The Coalition's economic strategy (running budget surpluses): Has it made a bad thing worse?' Oxford Economics UK Economic Outlook May 2014.

2. The dismissive comment about the significance of ONS revisions, by Rob Wood, chief UK economist at the German private bank Berenberg, was quoted by Katie Allen in the *Guardian*, 1st July 2014.

3. In addition to questioning the Coalition's stated reasons for the deficit reduction strategy, the economist Michael Lloyd produced a pithy document in December 2012, entitled *Ten Current Economic Untruths*. Typical was the following: we need a 'cap' on the social / welfare budget.

    Answer: We don't. Pension provision is 55 per cent of the budget and is not welfare. Housing benefit goes to landlords and should be controlled by private rent control. Disability benefits are just what they say and should not be cut. Other benefits are small and vary with the economic cycle, e.g. Unemployment benefit.

CHAPTER 15

BUBBLING HOUSE PRICES

ECONOMIC GROWTH brings budget deficits down, as Britain's experience in 2014 demonstrated. The austerity policy manifestly delayed the recovery, yet as we have seen this did not prevent the Chancellor and his Coalition colleagues from proclaiming that the policy had been necessary to the recovery. This absurd claim was well challenged by the biographer of Keynes, Lord Skidelsky, when addressing a gathering organised by the Official Monetary and Financial Institutions Forum think-tank in April 2014.

Lord Skidelsky reminded his audience of the fallacy known as *post hoc ergo propter hoc* which, loosely translated, means that something has occurred as a result of something that occurred before. The fallacy is to deduce that because the second event came after the first, it was therefore caused by it.

Again, the Coalition could hardly refrain from boasting that, at a growth rate of 3 per cent per annum in the first half of 2014, the British economy was expanding faster than any other member of the Group of Seven leading industrial nations. As another distinguished Keynesian, the Harvard economist Lawrence Summers pointed out: "While recent growth has been rapid, this is only because of the depth of the hole Britain dug for itself." With a year to go before the 2015 election, the UK's GDP was only just reaching its pre-crisis peak, whereas the US, which did not make the mistake of starting to with-draw the fiscal stimulus too soon, was by now recording output well above its previous peak. One should not be too impressed by rates of growth when levels of output are so depressed.

Apologists for the Coalition point to the way the squeeze was not as severe as originally intended, so that, although the budget deficit was falling, it was still greater than what earlier forecasts were pointing to as likely to be recorded by 2014. Professor Summers, a former US Treasury Secretary, neatly summarised the British growth record in 2014 as reflecting "a combination of the depth of the hole it found itself in, the moderation in the trend towards ever deeper austerity and the effects of possibly bubble-inducing government loans."

A fashionable investment in the UK in recent years has been 'buying (in order) to let'. Letting is especially profitable in London. This author can assure you, dear reader, that hardly a day goes by without our receiving a card through the door from a letting agent, with suggestions that we let our house to assorted corporations for the purpose of offering accom-modation to their executives. It appears that at least some of the subsidies offered by the government as part of the Help to Buy initiative were used by rich investors who were buying existing properties 'to let', with little impact on the more urgent task of building more houses. At all events, from the macro-economic point of view, the Help to Buy scheme seems, as Professor Summers deduced, to have made its contribution to the property price bubble which began to concern the Bank of England's Monetary Policy Committee and its Financial Policy Committee.

This is not to say that there was not some revival in house building during 2013 – the first year of real growth since the crisis. Thus Sir Charles Bean, the Deputy Governor of the Bank of England responsible for monetary policy, and formerly its Chief Economist, noted in an important speech in March 2014 that consumer spending increased by 2.2 per cent during

2013, while housing investment rose by 10 per cent. "Together, these two factors accounted for around two-thirds of the rise in activity." The key element was consumer spending, which accounts for some two-thirds of GDP. Moreover, the calculation for housing investment includes not only construction but the somewhat amorphous "value added in the facilitation of housing transactions" – i.e. it includes the buying and selling of existing houses, which does not do much to alleviate the housing shortage. The number of new houses on which construction had begun was still 25 per cent below the average in the pre-crisis decade, and the low level of house building in those days was one of the reasons for the chronic shortage of housing in more recent years. Moreover, when the Cabinet finally woke up to the housing crisis in 2014 it discovered that until new measures were taken, housing starts were due to be even lower that year than in 2013.

Sir Charles Bean spoke of "a risk that increased demand for housing ends up mainly in higher house prices rather than more houses, given the British problem with planning restrictions and the like" – a reference one assumes to the practice noted earlier of developers who hoard potential building land, even when they have planning permission.

The Bank was not the only institution to become concerned so early in the recovery about "excessive expansion in mortgage lending" and threats, once again, to financial stability. Bean's warning had been followed by a succession of his colleagues sounding the alarm, before the Paris-based Organisation for Economic Cooperation and Development waded in early in May.

Dating from the days when its predecessor was founded during the age of immediate post-war austerity to coordinate economic reconstruction in Europe, the OECD now boasts a membership of over 34 'market economies' throughout the world. Among other things it is an extremely powerful and respected research organisation, with an inside track to the statistics and thinking of member governments.

The OECD saw the UK's economic recovery gathering momentum, and raised its forecast for growth during 2014 from 2.4 per cent to 3.2 per cent – a small figure, but suggesting a quite dramatic increase. It stated in no uncertain terms that the government and Bank should be thinking hard about using those 'macro-prudential tools' to calm the housing market, with 'tighter controls' on mortgage lending. But whereas for a long time Governor Carney had evidently seen such controls as an alternative to raising interest rates, the OECD was reported as saying "the prospect of an imminent rise in interest rates must be clearly communicated to households."

In advocating measures to cool down the housing market the OECD was obviously thinking of price levels rather than the rate of activity in house building where, as Bean had pointed out, there was still a long way to catch up. Indeed, in contrast to the way that housing starts were still some 25 per cent below the average of the pre-crisis decade, house prices in the UK were on average already above the pre-crisis peak, a distinction being made between London, where prices were no less than 20 per cent above pre-crisis levels in the first quarter of 2014, and the rest of the UK, where they were 2 per cent below.

The contrast between the movements of the prices of houses and the number of houses being built could hardly have been starker. The 'rebalancing' problems of the British economy were still formidable after four years of Mr Osborne's Chancellorship. In many ways, this had actually been aggravated rather than alleviated by his concentration on 'austerity'.

Notes

1. Professor Summers was writing in the *Financial Times*, to which he is a regular and highly valued contributor, on 24th

May 2014, in an article appropriately entitled: UK austerity is no model for the world.

2. Sir Charles Bean, during the last few months of his stint as deputy governor, gave an important speech on the future of monetary policy on 21st March 2014, from which the quotations in this chapter are taken. Later, on the brink of his retirement, he spoke on 30th June 2014 of the possibility of Bank Rate rising one day to 5 per cent – somewhat above the 3 per cent ceiling to which Governor Carney had frequently alluded.

CHAPTER 16

INTEREST RATE DILEMMAS

IN SOME MODERN economic treatises there are so many statistics and equations that meaningful words appear few and far between. In this contemporary account I have tried to keep the use of statistics to a minimum, and, in addition to criticising the policy of what I regard as needless austerity, I have attempted to deal with various aspects of economic policy that people often raise with me.

Now and again, however, there are some statistics – or 'numbers' as analysts like to say – which are so striking that they are worth emphasising. While I was writing the previous chapter, with its reference to the government's Help to Buy scheme, there was so much coverage of it, and concern expressed in the press, that one would almost have concluded that it was the principal factor behind the rapid rise in house prices, and the 'bubble' that was becoming a big talking point. The climax of the criticism came with the news that no fewer than three former Chancellors, all Conservatives, had given the same advice to the Chancellor, namely that it was time to rein in the Help to Buy scheme.

It was therefore fascinating to discover that, while unveiling its latest assessment of the economy, with the hot news that in March the level of GDP had finally returned to within a whisker of its pre-recession peak, the National Institute of

133

Economic and Social Research (NIESR) stated that, according to its calculations, the Help to Buy scheme had accounted for less than 2 per cent of the 1.1 million transactions in the housing market since its inception in April 2013. Much more important was the cheapness of mortgages and the wider availability of credit after the credit contraction was followed by the expansionary policy towards credit and the money supply known as 'quantitative easing'.

The impact of the Help to Buy scheme was therefore marginal, although it has to be remembered that economists are always interested in what happens 'at the margin'. Again, the popular impression that the stimulus to the recovery of consumer spending came principally from a return to borrowing was challenged by Sir Charles Bean: the Bank's analysis showed that with real incomes depressed in 2013–14, the main impetus to spending came from a reduction in people's savings. But the forecasts of continued, indeed accelerating, recovery made by the Bank, the Office for Budget Responsibility and the NIESR all assumed rising real incomes from the spring of 2014 onwards as well as further reduction in savings.

However, although the NIESR calculated that the British economy was finally back, in terms of output, to its pre-crisis peak, as noted, this partly reflected the growth in the population since then. The Director of the NIESR, Jonathan Portes, said it would be some years before per capita incomes would be back to their previous peak.

Moreover, it had been the slowest recovery from recession on record – slower even than the recovery from the Great Depression of 1929–31, which took two years fewer than in 2008–14. In the US, where there had been a larger, more prolonged Keynesian stimulus than in the UK, GDP in May 2014 was already 6.5 per cent above the pre-crisis peak, although even that recovery did not satisfy critics such as Paul Krugman, who had called for a more substantial and prolonged stimulus. And, incidentally, the budget deficit position in the

US was improving faster than in the UK, thanks, surprise, surprise, to faster growth.

Many people were becoming concerned in the first half of 2014 about the higher levels of debt. The Chancellor took comfort from statistics showing that, although the level was worrying people, the debt to GDP ratio was lower, at 140 per cent, than at the peak of the boom, when it had been 174 per cent. Governor Carney appeared to derive less comfort from this comparison.

One problem was, as noted, the unbalanced relationship between fiscal and monetary policy. This stemmed from the decision to concentrate on fiscal austerity which George Osborne took right at the beginning of his tenure of office; this commitment to austerity was reinforced in October 2013 and the Budget of March 2014.

Earlier I compared the workings of monetary policy to, at one extreme, pushing on a string, and, at the other, a sudden catapulting of a credit-fuelled economy. Mr Carney had spoken of 'escape velocity'. Professor Summers used the metaphor of a 'coiled spring'. Certainly, after almost three years of 'flatlining', the British economy had sprung into action in 2014, apparently, to mix the metaphor, firing on all cylinders. Jonathan Portes of the NIESR, who, like me, had used the word 'depression' to describe the 2010–12 period, was now presenting forecasts of 2.9 per cent growth for 2014, and 2.4 per cent for both 2015 and 2016. He envisaged that there was plenty of spare capacity to sustain this.

As far as Chancellor Osborne was concerned, the good growth figures were very much in accordance with what he claimed to be his 'long-term plan'. In an interview on the BBC's 'Today' programme to celebrate the return to pre-crisis levels, Mr Osborne began to shift the emphasis from the budgetary strategy to an issue that has concerned this author for some time, namely the need for Britain 'to pay its way in the world'.

Here we return to the balance of payments and the balance of policy.

Whereas the resumption of economic growth was easing the budgetary figures, it was also likely to exacerbate the underlying balance of payments problem. As noted, the economy had been recording deficits equivalent to 5 per cent of GDP. But the emphasis on public spending cuts had put the burden of macroeconomic policy on cheap money, and now there was more and more concern about asset prices and the need to tighten monetary policy via higher interest rates.

What, among other things, was the prospect of higher interest rates likely to do? The answer, other things being equal, was almost certainly to strengthen the pound even further – a pound that had already risen by 10 per cent on average against other currencies during the previous year. This had to mean that a third of the adjustment made to the exchange rate during 2007–09 had been reversed. And, although there were occasional suggestions that 'devaluation no longer works', it did appear that the trade position had at least been prevented from getting even worse as a result of that devaluation. The possible impact of a rise in interest rates on the value of sterling was undoubtedly one of Carney's concerns.

For Britain to 'pay its way' in the world, a further rise in the value of sterling, with its impact on the competitiveness of exports, while making imports cheaper, was not exactly what the economic doctor ordered. But the logic of a policy that depended on a relaxed monetary policy and a tight fiscal policy pointed inexorably to a rise in interest rates to prick an asset price bubble.

Wherever I went in the spring of 2014 I found a spreading view that the Chancellor was relying on an old-fashioned pre-election boom, and that, whatever happened in the long run, a stronger pound would strengthen that famous 'feel good factor', both with regard to foreign holidays and the ability to buy cheaper imports after a long period when real incomes had been squeezed.

Notes

Most of the statistics cited in this chapter come from the National Institute of Economic and Social Research (NIESR) and / or from the NIESR director Jonathan Portes's regular BLOG.

An interesting point made in the NIESR's quarterly economic review in May 2014 was that the recovery since mid-2013 had been associated with a 'surge in spending on consumer durables, where the annual growth rate reached 9.7 per cent by the end of 2013.... (and) purchases of household appliances and motor vehicles were particularly buoyant.'

This seems to me to be a classic illustration of the view that economies do eventually recover, even if the recovery is delayed by bad macroeconomic policies. Both with regard to industrial investment and household investment, there comes a time when equipment needs to be replaced.

CONCLUSION

GEORGE OSBORNE'S economic experiment has been very political, and, to my mind, cynically calculated.

The new Chancellor arrived at the Treasury in June 2010 after the second cataclysm to hit the British economy in 70 years. The first was the Second World War, which left the British nation almost bankrupt, with precious few resources available for anything but the provision of the barest essentials for the population. There was, to coin a phrase, 'no alternative' to a period of genuine austerity, symbolised most of all by the continued distribution of wartime ration books.

The second cataclysm was the onset of what the then Managing Director of the IMF, Dominique Strauss-Kahn, called 'The Great Recession', which both Jonathan Portes, Director of the National Institute of Economic Research, and this author regarded as an out-and-out depression of economic activity. (Before moving to the Bank's Monetary Policy Committee, Portes's predecessor Martin Weale had also used the term 'depression'.)

There were other essential differences between the two periods to which the label 'austerity' came to be attached. The second cataclysm hit an economy in which the standard of living was already far, far higher than in 1945. Secondly, in this author's view, while there undoubtedly had to be a period of adjustment, the underlying economic situation did not require a period of austerity. On the contrary, it required budgetary policies to expand demand in the economy, not to cut it back even further. Moreover, while it is generally acknowledged by historians that the burden of austerity in 1945–51 was shared among all social layers of the population, by contrast, since 2010 the burden of 'cuts' which, it is argued in this book, were largely unnecessary, has fallen on the poorer members of society.

To make matters worse – and this is where I believe the charge of cynicism and political calculation is not without foundation – it became clear as the Coalition went on, that, at least from the Conservatives' point of view, cuts hitting the more vulnerable members of society were designed to finance reductions in taxation for the rest of the electorate. An early manifestation of this design was the Chancellor's decision to reduce the top rate of tax, which had been raised by the previous government, and was generally seen as a way of 'sharing the pain' of the adjustment to the financial crisis.

Despite its programme of 'austerity-driven' budgetary cuts, the government blissfully forecast in mid-2010 that there would soon be an economic recovery. Critics maintained that budgetary contraction was no way to promote such a recovery, and they – we – were right. The recovery that had begun in the first half of 2010 was arrested in its tracks. A period of what Ed Balls, the Shadow Chancellor, termed 'flatlining' ensued – although Balls's original perceptive analysis was made in August 2010, before he was actually appointed Shadow Chancellor. The 22nd June 2010 Budget forecast was for GDP growth of 2.3 per cent in 2011, 2.8 per cent in 2012 and 2.9 per cent in 2013. The outturn, according to Treasury figures published in June 2014 was respectively 1.1 per cent, 0.3 per cent and 1.7 per cent.

It is true that the budgetary squeeze was not quite as tight as intended; nevertheless, the squeeze over the next few years amounted to over 5 per cent of GDP – as the Chancellor actually boasted to his audience of right-wing Americans. As noted, economies recover eventually, if only because out-of-date items have to be replaced; but 'eventually' can, indeed, mean quite a long time in the teeth of a fiscal squeeze. Reliance was placed on monetary policy, which operates, in the celebrated words of Milton Friedman, with "long and variable lags".

Many people, including, possibly, the Chancellor himself, were misled by the fact that although Bank Rate was kept at a record low level for so long, yet a tangible recovery remained in the eyes and equations of the economic forecasters. What did not seem to be appreciated for a long time was that the stock of money and credit was in fact contracting. It was not until an aggressive programme of expansion of money and credit took place, under the weird description 'quantitative easing', that the position substantially changed. And, of course, QE was augmented by various governmental and Bank of England schemes to boost lending.

Monetary policy in the UK under the Chancellorship of George Osborne and the Governorships of first Mervyn, subsequently Lord, King and later Mark Carney, moved from a position where it was like pushing on a string, to acting almost like a catapult, or, in the metaphor of Professor Lawrence Summers, serving as if it were a spring that had suddenly been uncoiled.

The consequence, especially when people viewed the sharp rise in house prices, was to evoke memories of the financial instability that preceded the financial crisis of 2007–08, even though the economy was, by mid-2014, barely back to pre-crisis levels, and some 20 per cent below what might have been expected from historical trends.

George Osborne found himself in the interesting position of boasting to his Cabinet that he wanted an old-fashioned house price boom before the election, while relying on the Bank of England to keep it under some sort of control. In particular, the Chancellor was relying on Mark Carney, the Canadian central banker whom he had pursued, on and off, for a year in an eventually successful effort to persuade him to succeed Mervyn King in 2013.

The last thing the Chancellor wanted was a recrudescence of 'financial instability' before the next election. And the last thing he wanted from the Bank of England was a dramatic rise in interest rates should there be another boom in asset prices. In Mark Carney he had chosen a central banker who was on record well before his appointment as stressing the importance of macro-prudential measures, such as stringent capital requirements, to control lending, as a 'first line of defence'. He believed that stronger and more countercyclical capital requirements would "change the transmission mechanism and, consequently, the implementation of monetary policy".

The corollary of Carney's approach was that interest rates should not be the automatic monetary weapon to use against a boom in house and other asset prices, but should be kept in reserve. But it became increasingly clear in the first half of 2014 that Carney was concerned about the still high levels of consumer debt and the implications of yet another 'old-fashioned house price boom'; not to put too fine a point upon it, Carney began to cover himself should it all end in tears. When others on the Monetary Policy Committee and the Financial Policy Committee – both of which he chaired – were at least thinking about a possible need to raise interest rates, Carney alternated between being dovish and hawkish. He seemed to be laying a kind of paper trail, to demonstrate that, should everything go wrong, he had sounded enough warnings. Of particular note were his emphasis on the obvious point that the Bank of England might be responsible for financial stability, but not for house building, and his telling remark that Canada possessed half the population of the UK but built twice as many houses. This came shortly after the relatively new Deputy Governor of the Bank, the career civil servant Sir Jon Cunliffe – who had much experience of the Treasury and Number 10 Downing Street – made a widely noted speech in which he more or less warned 'here we go again' with regard to the boom in house prices.

Carney's was a very political appointment, by a very political Chancellor. To this author, at least, it began to look as though the Governor who had stressed the need for the UK economy to achieve 'escape velocity' was now considering an 'escape strategy' for his own reputation.

There was a wonderful paradox about Carney's position on interest rates. He rightly emphasised when presenting the Bank's May 2014 quarterly Inflation Report that the recovery was still in its early stages, implying that it would be a tragedy if premature action on interest rates were to abort the recovery. Indeed, many people would jokingly refer in private to 'this so-called recovery' (or words to that effect) and there was a strong undercurrent in banking, and legal circles, not least among insolvency practitioners, that 'over-borrowing' among businesses and households had been so prevalent in recent years that increases in the cost of borrowing could yet abort the recovery. As one insolvency practitioner put it to me: "These may yet be known as the years of Carney-age".

The paradox was that, from the point of view of many natural Conservative voters, not least those members of the much-talked about 'lucky generation', who had good pensions and were beneficiaries of the property boom, high interest rates would be 'good news'. Indeed, there was a sharp and understandable difference of perspective among those who did not wish to abort the recovery by raising rates, and people with savings and annuities offering them pitifully low returns. Sir Charles Bean of the Bank of England had made the point in one speech that he sympathised with those who were hit by low interest rates, but that monetary policy had to be set for the good of the wider economy. Nevertheless, the balance of economic policy, with a continued squeeze on the public sector – and another five years of austerity for the welfare budget if the Conservatives were re-elected – meant that fiscal policy had been excessively tight, and monetary policy, correspondingly, excessively loose.

Behind it all was, in my view, a mistaken strategy of adding unnecessarily to the downward pressure on the economy in the early stages. Of course the emphasis on austerity did not cause the crisis. The point is that it aggravated the crisis, delayed the recovery, and took the form of planned penury for the already vulnerable who became the scapegoat for a crisis that had little to do with them.

The better-off continued to receive tax relief on their pension contributions, and such benefits as winter fuel allowance and free bus passes were still available, although child benefit was restricted above a certain level. I myself have always accepted the argument made by Sir Ian Gilmour many years ago that the principle of universal benefits was a good one – an aspect, to coin a phrase, of 'all being in it together' – and that taxation of child benefit above a certain level preserved the universal principle. However, that battle has been lost.

I am not therefore arguing that the austerity rules should have applied to such benefits, but making the point that the principal losers from the austerity programme were those at the lower end of the income scale, where benefits were either cut or raised by less than the increase in the retail prices index. The government made a point of arguing that the top 10 per cent of income earners had lost ground: but, as the Child Poverty Action Group pointed out, the lowest 20 per cent suffered markedly from tax and benefit changes amounting to some £20bn extra a year. The main need for social services is felt by the poorest, and they are hit most by, for example, the closure of 'Sure Start' centres. Moreover, whatever relative losses the top 10 per cent might have experienced in the tables of 'income distribution', they more than made up from the inflation of asset prices when it came to measures such as the Sunday Times 'Wealth List'.

The hole in the argument justifying the attack on the welfare programme as a means of reducing the deficit was provided by the Prime Minster and Chancellor themselves, when they declared their plans for tax cuts and a smaller state. It was not the deficit alone that they were interested in, although they do seem to have fooled a lot of the people a lot of the time with their emphasis on deficit reduction per se. It is also, sadly, a sign of just how pervasive the neo-liberal movement has been in recent decades that the Opposition Labour Party also found it necessary to bow to the fashionable cry for 'cuts' when the level of GDP was barely back to its pre-crisis level and some 20 per cent below what historic trends would have pointed to.

In 1976, during the IMF crisis which afflicted the Callaghan government, the civil servant in charge of controlling public expenditure at the Treasury was Sir Leo Pliatzki. He subsequently wrote a book entitled Getting and Spending – a title derived from Wordsworth. In common with most other 'Keynesians' he made the distinction between the obvious need to raise revenue to finance public expenditure, and the importance of fiscal policy for the management of demand in the economy.

When businesses and consumers collectively cut back their spending after the onset of the financial crisis of 2007–08, it was for the government to fill the hole in the economy as over-indebted households tried to sort out their finances. The banking crisis itself led to a contraction of money and credit which served to aggravate the situation. Economic growth will gradually bring down the deficit. But the question society has to ask itself is that, in normal times, does it want a reasonable standard of public services, in which case the level of taxation has to reflect that demand, or is it really happy with the neo-liberal desire for ever lower tax rates, at the expense of public services in general and the welfare of the poor in particular?

Notes

1. A very detailed, and disturbing, account of the impact of the austerity policy on the more vulnerable is contained in *Hard Times – The Divisive Toll Of The Economic Slump* (2014) by Tom Clark with Anthony Heath.

2. While completing these footnotes, I found myself moved by a remark made by Gordon Brown in an interview in the *Guardian*, 1st September 2014. 'I dislike intensely everything the Tories have done. I hate the bedroom tax. I feel the cuts in social security benefits are heinous at a time when they are cutting tax for the very rich. I feel very angry that poverty is rising in this country.'

   This from a man who, as Chancellor, saw his role as 'using the levers of economic power to get children out of poverty and to give families better chances and to help people get employment opportunities and to deliver people from poverty on old age.'

3. My final footnote is from the round-robin I received from my neighbour, the Liberal David Gladstone (yes, he is a relation of the Treasury's 19th century hero), at Christmas 2013. It strikes a chord.

   'Sharing as I do the Whigs' Belief in Progress, I am disappointed that our current Leaders should have fallen back on the punitive approach to Welfare which two Centuries ago resulted in those judged by Overseers to be workshy being pilloried in the Stocks; and, a Century later, in the creation of the Work-houses whose Cruelties were so vividly exposed by Mr Charles Dickens. Just as the Poor are always with us, so, I fear, are those that scent political and pecuniary profit in Poverty.'

Postscript

After I had completed this book, the Office for National Statistics (ONS) published lots of revisions to the figures for gross domestic product in recent years. One bizarre aspect was that the 'output' of the drug trade and prostitution had been added to the totals.

There were many other 'revisions'. However, the new figures do not substantially alter the picture painted in this book. In this context, it is worth quoting comments by the ONS chief economist, Joe Grice, on Wednesday 3rd September, 2014:

"Despite the wide-ranging improvements underpinning the new estimates, the broad picture has not changed much. Although the downturn was less deep than previously estimated and subsequent growth stronger, the UK experienced the deepest recession since ONS records began in 1948 and the subsequent recovery has been unusually slow."

INDEX

Adonis, Andrew 43
Attlee, Clement 12, 35, 80
American Enterprise Institute 5, 87, 93, 97, 98 119
American loan 2, 21, 22, 25, 27, 39,

Balls, Ed 39, 49, 65, 75, 77, 81, 82, 140
Bank bonuses 49, 50, 55
Bank of England 40–5, 49, 53, 56–8, 62–5, 67, 75, 86, 87, 90, 99,
    100, 104, 105, 108, 117, 119, 123, 126, 139, 140, 141
Banking crisis of 2007-08 2, 57, 67, 77, 88, 89, 95, 143
'Barber boom' 108
Barclays 50
Barings 49, 53
BBC 135
BCCI 53
Bean, Sir Charles 128, 131, 134, 143
Bernanke, Ben 55–7, 88
Beveridge Report 27
Bevin, Ernest 23
'Black Wednesday' 26, 90
Blair, Tony 49, 122
Blanchard Olivier 96
Blunden, Sir George 105
Bretton Woods 19, 20–2, 25, 34
Bridges, Lord 22

'Britain Isn't Working' 105
British Empire 20
Brittan, Sir Samuel 72, 78
Brown, Gordon 4, 7, 40, 41, 45, 48, 53, 65, 77, 113, 144, 150
Bundesbank 115
Business cycle 79
Byrne, Liam 15

Cairncross, Sir Alec 23, 35
Callaghan, James 15, 70
Cameron, David 1, 40, 63, 92, 99, 114
Canada 5, 43, 44, 49, 142
Carney, Mark 42, 49, 58, 97, 106, 109, 116, 121, 131, 135, 143
Catholic Cardinal Archbishop of Westminster 99
Centre for Business Research 110
Child Poverty Action Group 3, 144
China 42, 46
Chote, Robert 59, 99, 108, 124
Coalition Government (in UK 2010 -) 1, 6, 12, 46, 73
Citizen's Advice Bureau 3
City University 53
Churchill, Winston 15, 18, 21
Clark, Tom 146
Clarke, Kenneth 48, 70
Coalition government 1
Commodity prices 46, 47
Confederation of British Industry (CBI) 108
Conservative Party 7, 89, 108, 109, 122
Copernicus 78
Covent Garden 12
Cripps, Sir Stafford 13, 14, 23, 26, 29, 34, 39
Cunliffe, Sir Jon 142

Daily Mail 63
Daily Telegraph 63

Dalton, Hugh 18, 23, 24, 27, 39, 40
Darling, Alistair 40, 47
Dow, Christopher 23-24
Deflation 58, 73, 74, 77, 78, 83
Depression of 1929-32
'Deregulation culture' 50
Devaluation (of 1949) 25
Dickens, Charles 146

Economic Club of New York 100
Eden, Anthony 97
Elliott, Larry 108
Eurozone 59, 65
Exchange controls 18, 22
Exchange rate policy 113, 117
Exchange Rate Reform Group 117

Federal Reserve Board 50
Feinstein, Charles 25
Fildes, Christopher 56
Financial Times 5, 50, 72, 74, 88, 116, 130
Financial regulation 49, 55
    'light touch approach' 49
Fiscal policy 151
First World War 14
Food Banks (in UK) 3, 122
France 115
Friedman, Milton 43, 72, 141

Gaitskell, Hugh 31
Galbraith JK 106
General Theory of Employment, Interest and Money 78
German Finance Ministry 115
Germany 20, 88, 89, 115
Gilmour, Ian 144

Gladstone, William 88, 92
Globalisation 4
Goldman Sachs 50
Goodhart, Charles 92
Gordon, Robert 100
Greece 99
Greenspan, Alan 79
Grice, Joe 147
Group of 7 (G7) 4, 46
Guardian 63, 108, 125, 146

Harris, Kenneth 34
Harrison, Dr Rupert 45
Harrod, Roy 16, 35
Healey, Denis 113, 123
Heath, Sir Edward 107, 108
'Help to Buy' 128, 133, 134
Hennessy, Peter 35
Henry, Professor Brian 122, 125
Heseltine, Michael 91
How to Pay for the War 19
Hull, Cordell 17

ICI 89
Imperial Preference 17
Institute for Fiscal Studies 3, 59
International Monetary Fund (IMF) 6, 59, 66, 70, 81, 89, 96, 97,
    101, 102, 121
Interest rates 5, 42, 43, 45, 55, 67, 81, 89, 101, 107, 109, 111–3, 116,
    121, 130, 136, 142, 143
Ireland 120
'Irrational Exuberance' 79
Italy 114
Japan 78
Jenkins, Anthony 50

Johnson, Boris 63, 92, 93
Johnson Matthey Bankers 53
Joseph Rowntree Trust 3

Kahn, Richard 61
Kaldor, Lord 92
Keynes, JM 2, 16, 21, 61, 64, 70, 71, 72, 106
Keynesians 152
Kindleberger, Charles 35, 87
King, Mervyn 54, 56, 64, 65, 141, 142
Kinnock, Neil 14
Korean War 27
Krugman, Paul 58, 61, 96, 134
Kynaston, David 34

Labour Party 24
'Labour's Mess', the myth of 40, 46, 48, 57, 69, 100
Lansbury, George 12, 13
Laws, David 15
Lawson, Nigel 113
Leeson, Nick 49
Lloyd, Michael 125
Le Carré, John
Lend Lease 16, 17, 18, 21
Liberal Democrat Party 15, 16
'Living wage' 104
Lloyd, Michael 122
Lothian, Lord 17
Lyons, Dr Gerard 41

Macmillan, Harold 33
Macpherson, Sir Nicholas 49, 51, 66
Mais lecture 53, 116
Major, John 48, 69
government of 48

Malthus, Thomas 100
Marshall Plan 2, 23, 25, 35, 39
Martin, Bill 108, 110
Marx, Karl 111
McKinsey and Company 54
Milward Alan 25
Moggridge D.E. 18
Monetary Policy 87
Money supply 57, 58, 72, 81, 134
Monetary policy 128, 131, 135, 136, 141–4
Monetary Policy Committee (MPC) 56, 78, 107, 112, 128, 142
Multiplier, The 58, 61, 74

National Health Service (NHS) 27, 29, 82
Neild, Robert 4
National Institute of Economic and Social Research (NIESR)
    7, 11, 125, 133, 137
New York Economic Club 96
New York Times 123
North Sea Oil 91

Office for National Statistics 3
Organisation for Economic Co-operation and Development
    (OECD) 25, 41, 129
Office for Budget Responsibility 5, 46, 59, 65, 67, 103, 110, 114,
    124, 134
Oil shocks of 1970s 89
Olivier, Sir Laurence 30
Official Monetary and Financial Institutions Forum (OMFIF)
    127,
Open Market Operations (see Quantitative Easing)
Osborne, George 3, 27, 39, 58, 60, 83, 93, 95, 103, 107, 119, 122,
    135, 141
'Omnishambles' budget of 2012 95
Outsourcing 64

'Paradox of thrift' 78
Pasinetti, Luigi 61
Pliatzki, Sir Leo 145
Pöhl, Karl Otto 113
Portes, Jonathan 134-139
PSBR (Public Sector Borrowing Requirement) 67
Public Sector Deficits 3
Portugal 114
Prior, James 91

Quantitative Easing (QE) 56, 57, 72, 74, 81, 89, 141

Ramsden, Dave 74
Reagan, Ronald 49
Robinson, Joan 58
Roosevelt FD 17
Rowthorn, Bob 108

Schumpeter, Joseph 61
'Scroungers' 103
Second World War 2, 70, 78, 82, 90, 139
Shinwell, Emanuel 31
Skidelsky, Robert 35, 74, 127
Soho 12
Spain 114, 120
Strauss-Kahn, Dominique 66, 139
Summers, Larry 95, 127, 128, 130, 135, 141
'Sure Start' 144

Thatcher, Margaret 49, 91, 93, 105
Towers, Graham 43
Truman, President Harry 23
Tucker, Paul 66

US Treasury 20

Wall Street Journal 105
Weale, Martin 139
'Welfare scroungers' 62
White, Harry Dexter 19
Wilson, Harold 33
Wincott, Harold 88
Wisconsin 104
Wolf, Martin 5, 74, 99
Wood, Rob 125
World Bank 89

Zero Hours Contracts 103

Lightning Source UK Ltd.
Milton Keynes UK
UKOW04f1313200415

249960UK00002B/54/P